I0815061
This journal belongs to

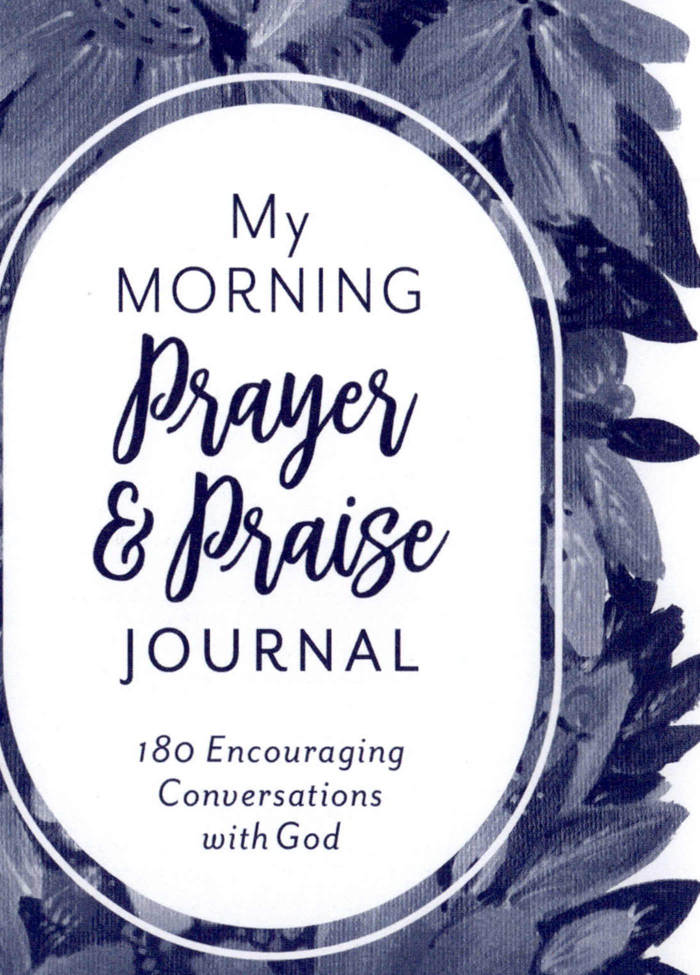

My MORNING Prayer & Praise JOURNAL

180 Encouraging Conversations with God

BARBOUR
PUBLISHING

© 2024 by Barbour Publishing, Inc.

ISBN 978-1-63609-729-9

Text compiled from *The 5-Minute Bible Study for Women, The 5-Minute Bible Study for Women: Mornings in God's Word, The 5-Minute Bible Study for the Less Stressed Life,* and *The 5-Minute Bible Study for Men: Mornings in God's Word.* All published by Barbour Publishing, Inc.

All rights reserved. No part of this publication may be reproduced or transmitted for commercial purposes, except for brief quotations in printed reviews, without written permission of the publisher. Reproduced text may not be used on the World Wide Web.

Churches and other noncommercial interests may reproduce portions of this book without the express written permission of Barbour Publishing, provided that the text does not exceed 500 words or 5 percent of the entire book, whichever is less, and that the text is not material quoted from another publisher. When reproducing text from this book, include the following credit line: "From *My Morning Prayer and Praise Journal*, published by Barbour Publishing, Inc. Used by permission."

Scripture quotations marked NIV are taken from the HOLY BIBLE, NEW INTERNATIONAL VERSION®. NIV®. Copyright © 1973, 1978, 1984, 2011 by Biblica, Inc.™ Used by permission. All rights reserved worldwide.

Scripture quotations marked NLT are taken from the *Holy Bible.* New Living Translation copyright© 1996, 2004, 2015 by Tyndale House Foundation. Used by permission of Tyndale House Publishers, Inc. Carol Stream, Illinois 60188. All rights reserved.

Scripture quotations marked NLV are taken from the New Life Version, copyright © 1969 and 2003 by Barbour Publishing, Inc., Uhrichsville, Ohio, 44683. All rights reserved.

Scripture quotations marked TLB are taken from The Living Bible © 1971. Used by permission of Tyndale House Publishers, Inc. Wheaton, Illinois 60189. All rights reserved.

Scripture quotations marked NASB are taken from the New American Standard Bible, © 1960, 1962, 1963, 1968, 1971, 1972, 1973, 1975, 1977, 1995, 2020 by The Lockman Foundation. Used by permission.

Scripture quotations marked NRSV are taken from the New Revised Standard Version Bible, copyright 1989, Division of Christian Education of the National Council of the Churches of Christ in the United States of America. Used by permission. All rights reserved.

Scripture quotations marked ESV are from The Holy Bible, English Standard Version®, copyright © 2001 by Crossway Bibles, a publishing ministry of Good News Publishers. The ESV ® text has been reproduced in cooperation with and by permission of Good News Publishers. Unauthorized reproduction of this publication is prohibited. All rights reserved.

Published by Barbour Publishing, Inc., 1810 Barbour Drive, Uhrichsville, Ohio 44683, www.barbourbooks.com

Our mission is to inspire the world with the life-changing message of the Bible.

Printed in China.

Introduction

Every morning you wake up, you have a choice to make. What tone will you set for today? Busy mornings aren't reserved for stay-at-home moms or women who work outside the home. The truth is that most of us are rushing through our first hours, just trying to make it to the next part of the day clean, dressed, and perhaps on time. But that frenzied process often leaves us stressed. And irritable. And impatient. Not a good way to start your day!

God has so much more in store for your days, friend!

This book is intended to help you begin your day in the very best place—at the throne of God, reading His Word and spending time in conversation with Him. It provides you with a place to journal your own thoughts, prayers, requests, and praises.

Pour yourself a cup of coffee and make the most of your mornings! You will find that even a few minutes focused on scripture and prayer has the power to make a huge difference. Soon you will want to make room for even more time with your loving heavenly Father!

Listen to my voice in the morning, Lord. Each morning I bring my requests to you and wait expectantly.

Psalm 5:3 NLT

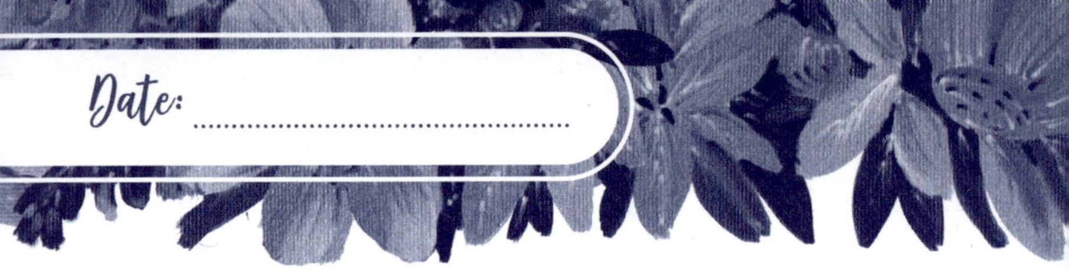

READ ROMANS 12

Do not conform to the pattern of this world,
but be transformed by the renewing of your mind.
Romans 12:2 niv

Father, I admit most days I feel more ordinary than extraordinary. But You call me to greatness, not because of what I can achieve but because of Your holiness and Your unending love for me. Each day I aspire to be more like You: more extraordinary than the day before. Amen.

prayer requests

praises

READ JOHN 14:1–27

"I am leaving you with a gift—peace of mind and heart! And the peace I give isn't fragile like the peace the world gives. So don't be troubled or afraid."

John 14:27 TLB

God, forgive me for not trusting You enough. Forgive me for placing my faith in what the world offers. I'm grateful for the gift of peace in a stressful world, and I'm committed to placing my faith in You above all else. Amen.

prayer requests

praises

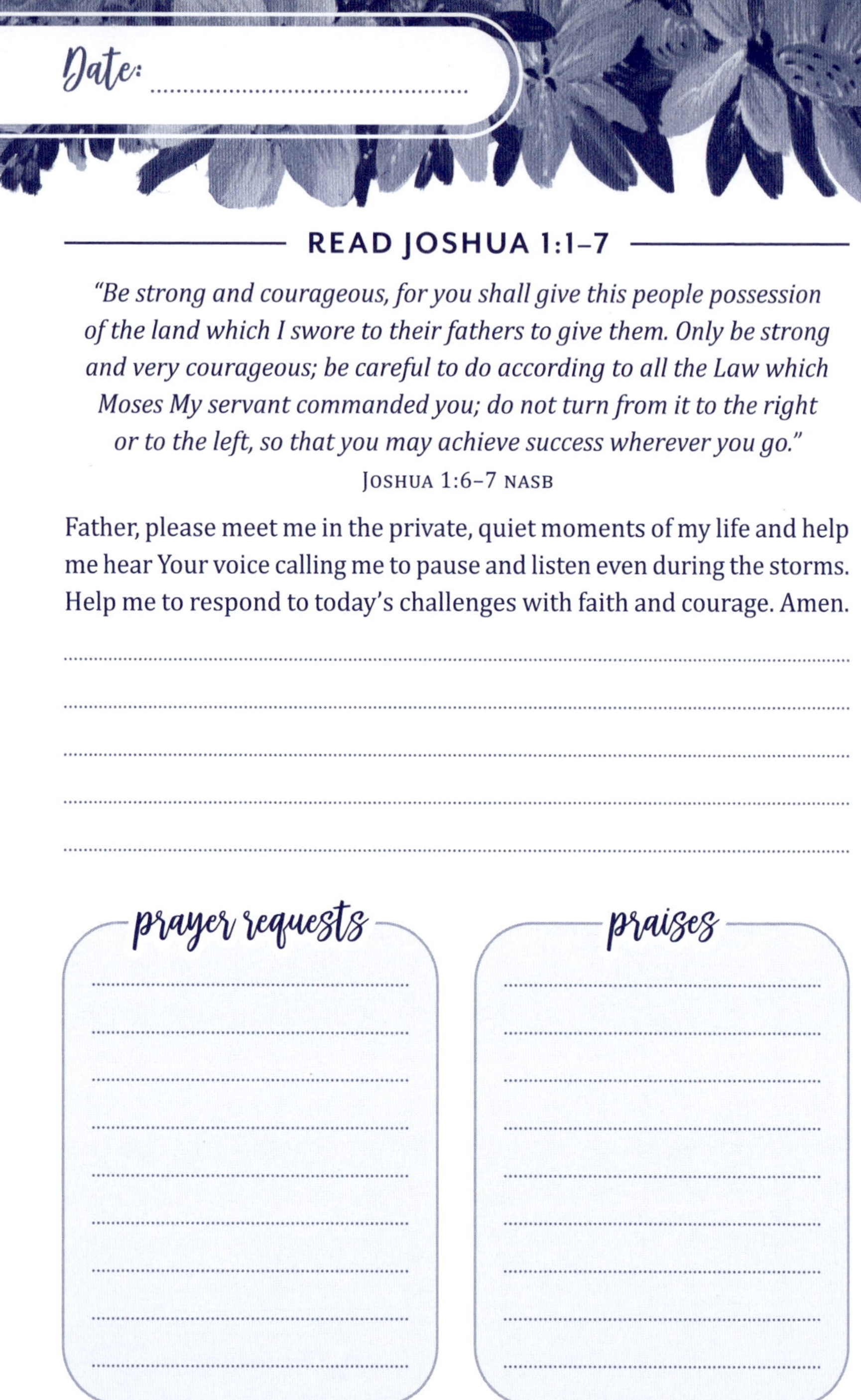

Date:

READ JOSHUA 1:1–7

"Be strong and courageous, for you shall give this people possession of the land which I swore to their fathers to give them. Only be strong and very courageous; be careful to do according to all the Law which Moses My servant commanded you; do not turn from it to the right or to the left, so that you may achieve success wherever you go."

JOSHUA 1:6–7 NASB

Father, please meet me in the private, quiet moments of my life and help me hear Your voice calling me to pause and listen even during the storms. Help me to respond to today's challenges with faith and courage. Amen.

prayer requests

praises

READ PSALMS 113:1–114:8

He raises the poor from the dust, He lifts the needy from the garbage heap, to seat them with noblemen, with the noblemen of His people.

Psalm 113:7–8 NASB

Lord, You are able to turn things around in our lives. Psalm 113 states that You give barren women children. You seat the poor at Your table as guests. Thank You for loving us so. Amen.

prayer requests

praises

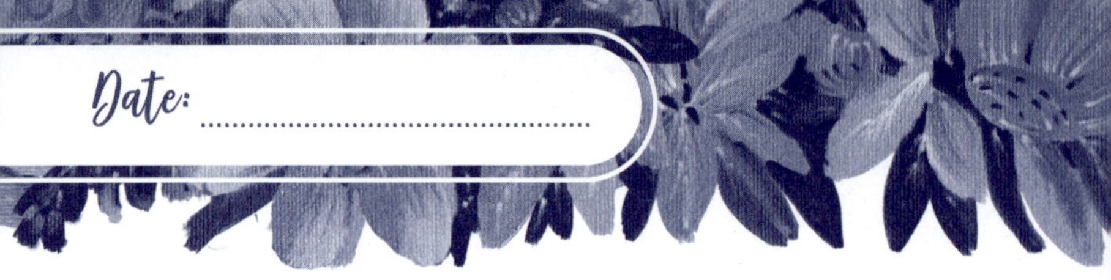

READ JEREMIAH 29:1–23

"For I know the plans I have for you," says the LORD. "They are plans for good and not for disaster, to give you a future and a hope."

JEREMIAH 29:11 NLT

God, I give my future to You. Forgive me for acting as if I am in control, because I'm not. You're much better at it. I believe You have good plans for my today and my tomorrows. Align my desires with Your will so that I am living today and every day in You. Please be the Lord of my life, Father. Amen.

prayer requests

praises

READ PSALM 55:1–23

Cast your cares on the LORD, and he will sustain you;
he will never let the righteous be shaken.
PSALM 55:22 NIV

God, I'm leaving my troubled heart with You and asking for a courageous heart instead. The idea of speaking up for justice brings on stress, so I'm depending on You to direct me in the when and how as I follow Your lead. Amen.

prayer requests

praises

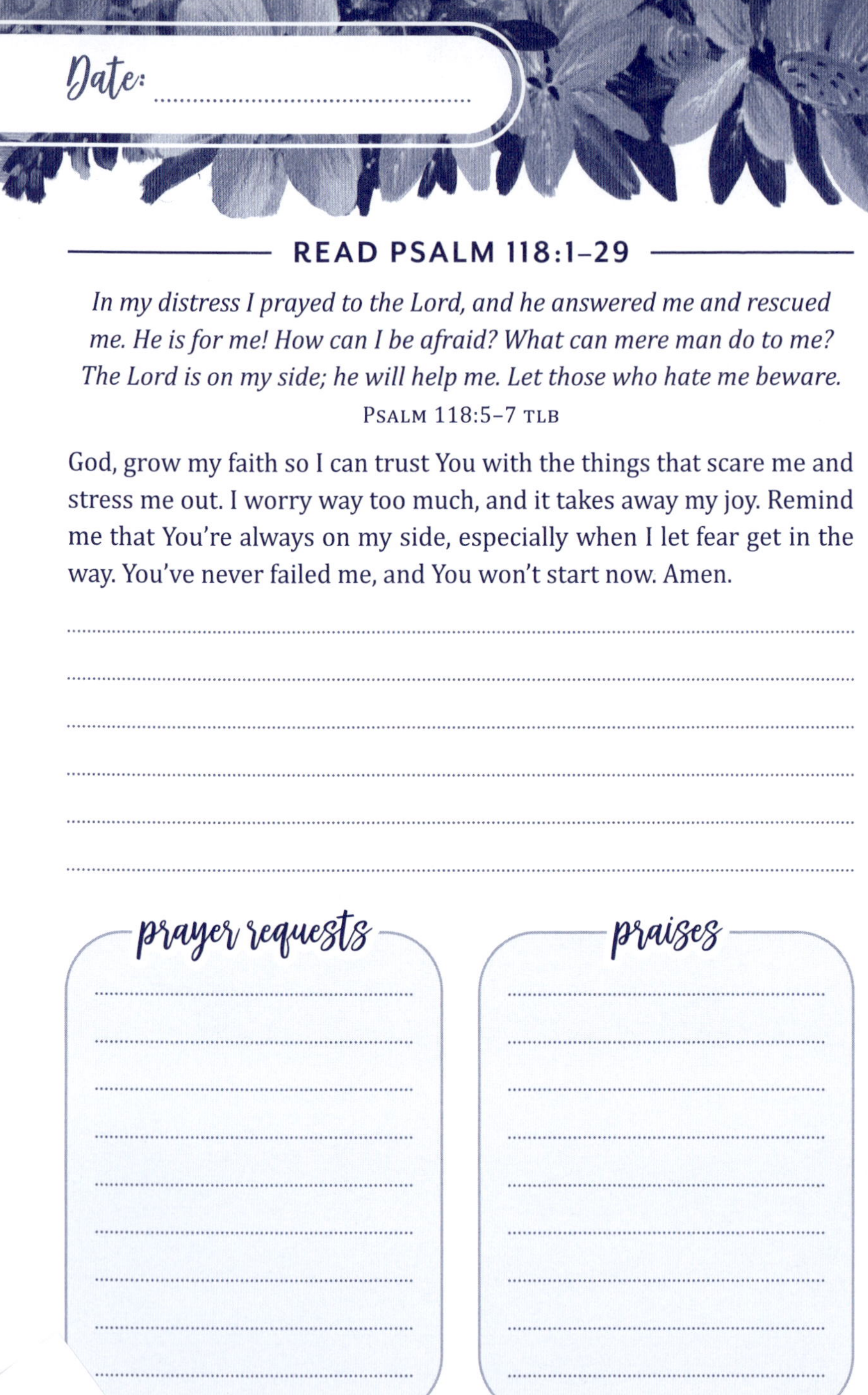

Date:

READ PSALM 118:1–29

In my distress I prayed to the Lord, and he answered me and rescued me. He is for me! How can I be afraid? What can mere man do to me? The Lord is on my side; he will help me. Let those who hate me beware.

Psalm 118:5–7 TLB

God, grow my faith so I can trust You with the things that scare me and stress me out. I worry way too much, and it takes away my joy. Remind me that You're always on my side, especially when I let fear get in the way. You've never failed me, and You won't start now. Amen.

prayer requests

praises

READ GALATIANS 5:13–18

For you have been called to live in freedom, my brothers and sisters. But don't use your freedom to satisfy your sinful nature. Instead, use your freedom to serve one another in love. For the whole law can be summed up in this one command: "Love your neighbor as yourself."

GALATIANS 5:13–14 NLT

Holy Spirit, thank You for Your presence in my life and for Your compassion for me. Help me to see the ways I can think of others and use my freedom to love and serve them. May I see the dead ends of personal indulgence today so that I can remain free in You. Amen.

prayer requests

praises

READ PSALM 139

For you created my inmost being; you knit me together in my mother's womb. I praise you because I am fearfully and wonderfully made; your works are wonderful, I know that full well.

Psalm 139:13–14 niv

Who am I, Father? I've put on so many masks over the years that I'm not sure I know my true self. But You accept me (Romans 15:7), call me Your friend (John 15:15), Your beloved child (Romans 8:17), and You set me free from sin (Galatians 5:1). Today I choose to be known. Reveal to me Your wisdom through Your Word. I want to know You more. Amen.

prayer requests

praises

READ 1 PETER 4:1–11

If anyone speaks, they should do so as one who speaks the very words of God. If anyone serves, they should do so with the strength God provides, so that in all things God may be praised through Jesus Christ. To him be the glory and the power for ever and ever.

1 Peter 4:11 niv

God, I know if I'm left to my own devices, I'll stay where I am, comfortable in my own little spot. Today I'm asking You to stretch me. Lead me boldly out of my comfort zone, and I will serve mightily for Your glory. Amen.

prayer requests

praises

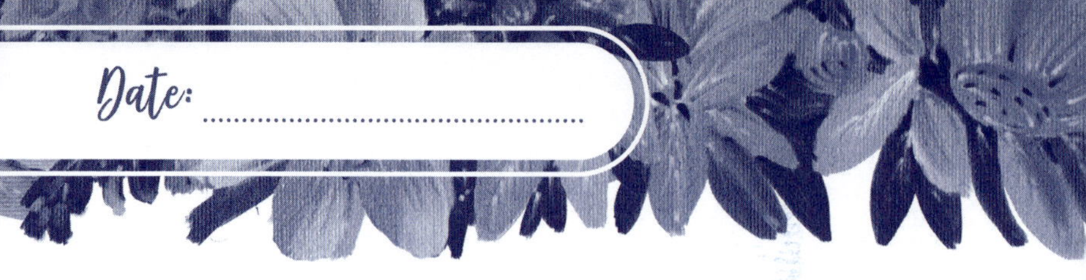

Date:

READ JAMES 1:1–15

God blesses those who patiently endure testing and temptation. Afterward they will receive the crown of life that God has promised to those who love him.

James 1:12 NLT

God, thank You for rewarding my faith. I know that You understand the struggles I face and how challenging obedience can be when I'm feeling overwhelmed by life. Grow my faith to trust You for the hope and healing I am desperate for. Amen.

prayer requests

praises

READ MATTHEW 6:1–8

"But when you pray, go into your room, close the door and pray to your Father, who is unseen. Then your Father, who sees what is done in secret, will reward you. And when you pray, do not keep on babbling like pagans, for they think they will be heard because of their many words."

MATTHEW 6:6–7 NIV

Father, I trust that You know what I need before I ask and that You will reward me for what I do for You and for others in secret. May I turn my gaze away from what I can gain from others right now and instead entrust myself to Your kindness and generosity as I pray. Amen.

prayer requests

praises

Date: ....

READ PHILIPPIANS 3:7–21

I focus on this one thing: Forgetting the past and looking forward to what lies ahead, I press on to reach the end of the race and receive the heavenly prize for which God, through Christ Jesus, is calling us.

PHILIPPIANS 3:13–14 NLT

Jesus, I'm forgetting about my past when I struggled to know my true goals from day to day. Now I'm running toward You. Give me the wisdom to continue in that race while I fulfill my daily responsibilities. I know when I am doing both, my life can and will glorify You! Amen.

prayer requests

praises

READ MATTHEW 10:24–31

"Are not two small birds sold for a very small piece of money? And yet not one of the birds falls to the earth without your Father knowing it. God knows how many hairs you have on your head. So do not be afraid. You are more important than many small birds."

MATTHEW 10:29–31 NLV

Father, sometimes I feel overlooked, unloved, and forgotten by others. I try not to dwell on it, but it hurts me deeply. Help me to remember that I am always in Your thoughts. You love me with a fierce love. When it comes down to it, God, You are all I need. Amen.

prayer requests

praises

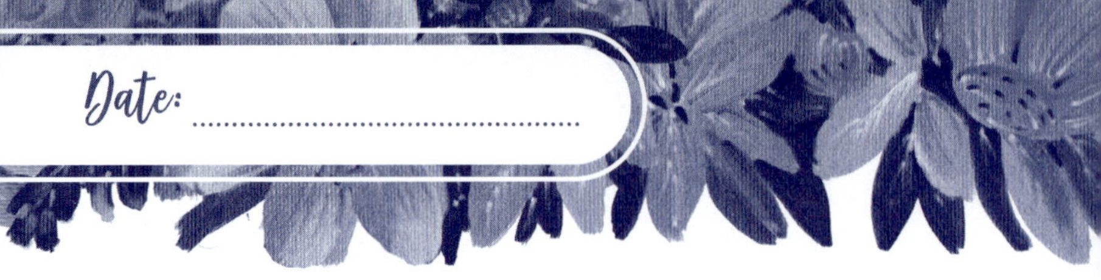

READ MATTHEW 6:19–34

"So don't worry about tomorrow, for tomorrow will bring its own worries. Today's trouble is enough for today."

MATTHEW 6:34 NLT

God, it is very hard for me to not worry about what's ahead. I see so many traps and pitfalls coming up, and I end up focusing on trying to figure out ways to avoid them. It robs me of being present with those I love. And it keeps me from trusting You. Please help me stay present so I can live in obedience to Your plan, believing You'll help me at the right time. Amen.

prayer requests

praises

READ PSALM 33:13–22

Our soul waits for the Lord; he is our help and shield. Our heart is glad in him, because we trust in his holy name. Let your steadfast love, O Lord, be upon us, even as we hope in you.

Psalm 33:20–22 NRSV

Father, You are greater than anyone or anything, and Your power is unmatched. May I find peace, hope, and gladness in Your presence and power today while I wait patiently for Your intervention in my life. May Your steadfast love rest on me and my loved ones. Amen.

prayer requests

praises

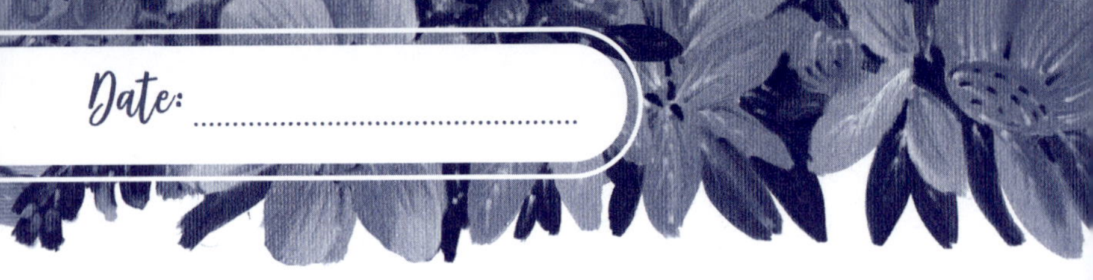

READ EXODUS 1:1–22

The midwives, however, feared God and did not do what the king of Egypt had told them to do; they let the boys live.

Exodus 1:17 NIV

Lord, thank You for the boldness of the two midwives who knew what the king ordered was wrong. They chose life! Thank You for the opportunities I have to do what is right even when it may be hard or frightening. May I be as bold as Shiphrah and Puah if following You becomes as dangerous for me as it was for them. Amen.

prayer requests

praises

READ ISAIAH 41:8–14

"For I have chosen you and will not throw you away.
Don't be afraid, for I am with you. Don't be discouraged,
for I am your God. I will strengthen you and help you.
I will hold you up with my victorious right hand."

Isaiah 41:9–10 NLT

Almighty God, no matter what I face, I know You are with me. You chose me for a reason, and I know You have a perfect plan for me safe inside Your will. Be near me, Father, especially when I am feeling unsure of the way. Hold me up when I can't stand on my own, and usher me into Your victorious presence forevermore. Amen.

prayer requests

praises

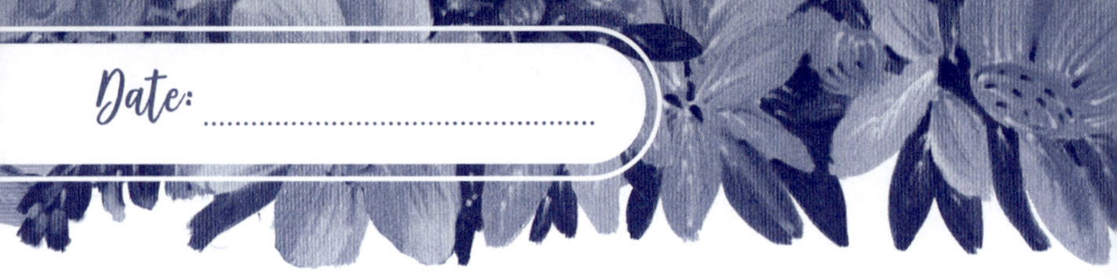

Date:

READ JOSHUA 1:1–18

"Yes, be bold and strong! Banish fear and doubt! For remember, the Lord your God is with you wherever you go."

JOSHUA 1:9 TLB

God, You ask hard things of me and sometimes I wish you didn't. But in my pursuit to live a less stressed life, I realize how important a relationship with You is. You're the one who makes righteous living possible. You're the one who adds the super to my natural so I can walk it out. Thank You for Your presence in my life. I love You! Amen.

prayer requests

praises

Date: ....

READ NEHEMIAH 1

"Remember, please, the word which You commanded Your servant Moses, saying, 'If you are unfaithful, I will scatter you among the peoples; but if you return to Me and keep My commandments and do them, though those of you who have been scattered were in the most remote part of the heavens, I will gather them from there and bring them to the place where I have chosen to have My name dwell.' "

NEHEMIAH 1:8–9 NASB

Father, You will not abandon Your people to their sins and failures if they repent and pray. I ask for Your mercy for my faults. May I show awareness and compassion to others who are suffering shame and deprivation today. Amen.

prayer requests

praises

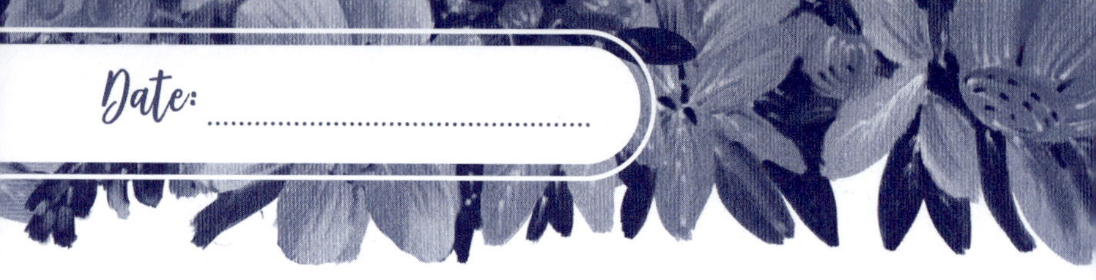

READ 1 THESSALONIANS 5:1–11

So encourage each other and build each other up, just as you are already doing.

1 Thessalonians 5:11 NLT

Father God, thank You for Your Word. The Bible as a whole and individual scriptures are such an encouragement to me. Today I am asking You to inhabit my words as I seek to encourage others the way You encourage me. Give me eyes to see those around me as You see them. Amen.

prayer requests

praises

READ PSALM 34

The L*ORD is near to the brokenhearted and saves the crushed in spirit. Many are the afflictions of the righteous, but the* L*ORD delivers him out of them all.*

PSALM 34:18–19 ESV

Lord of all my days, thank You for always being near. I love to celebrate with You when things are going well, but I am also deeply grateful that You come even closer when I am brokenhearted, grieving, and crushed in spirit. You are faithful to bring me through and are so patient with me when I am struggling. I don't deserve such kindness, but I am so thankful for it! Amen.

prayer requests

praises

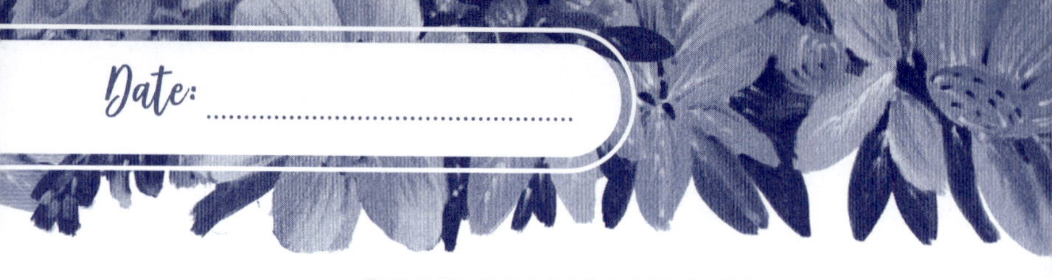

READ PSALM 103:1–22

He is merciful and tender toward those who don't deserve it; he is slow to get angry and full of kindness and love. He never bears a grudge, nor remains angry forever. He has not punished us as we deserve for all our sins, for his mercy toward those who fear and honor him is as great as the height of the heavens above the earth.

Psalm 103:8–11 TLB

God, You are amazing. I don't understand how You love me, especially with the ways I've messed up. I confess my stress and fear of You turning away from me. But now my heart is full of joy to know that's not the kind of God You are. I love You! Amen.

prayer requests

praises

READ DEUTERONOMY 8:1–10

"Yes, he humbled you by letting you go hungry and then feeding you with manna, a food previously unknown to you and your ancestors. He did it to teach you that people do not live by bread alone; rather, we live by every word that comes from the mouth of the LORD."

DEUTERONOMY 8:3 NLT

Father, You have promised to both humble me and to be present for me in life's challenges. May I learn to depend on You for my daily needs and care rather than relying on what I can control and what I can do on my own. I trust that You can provide for me in the most unlikely and unexpected ways. Amen.

prayer requests

praises

READ 1 SAMUEL 16:1–13

"The LORD doesn't see things the way you see them. People judge by outward appearance, but the LORD looks at the heart."

1 SAMUEL 16:7 NLT

God, I admit that I judge others unfairly. But I also know the unfairness of being judged by my appearance. Give me a beautiful heart overflowing with love, joy, peace, patience, kindness, goodness, faithfulness, and self-control. And if others see any beauty in me, let it be because of You. Amen.

prayer requests

praises

READ PSALM 149

Praise the Lord! Sing to the Lord a new song.
Sing his praises in the assembly of the faithful.
Psalm 149:1 NLT

God, I will sing praises to You when I awake and when I lie down at night—and every moment between. Give me a song in my heart and a melody on my lips to honor You with every note. Thank You for the gift of music and how it can touch my heart in such a powerful way. I am overwhelmed by Your goodness! Amen.

prayer requests

praises

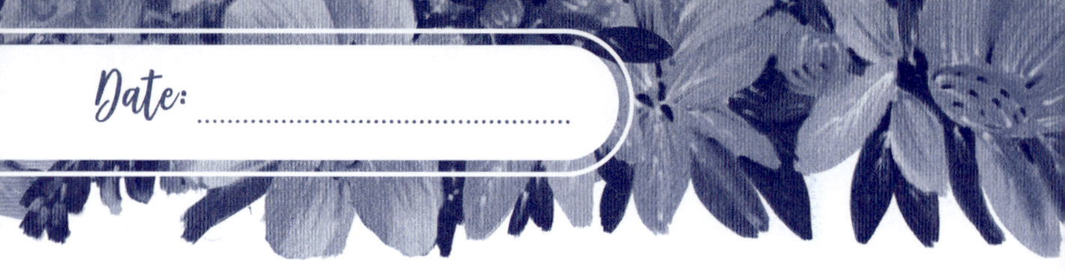

READ 1 JOHN 4:7–21

And as we live in God, our love grows more perfect. So we will not be afraid on the day of judgment, but we can face him with confidence because we live like Jesus here in this world. Such love has no fear, because perfect love expels all fear. If we are afraid, it is for fear of punishment, and this shows that we have not fully experienced his perfect love.

1 John 4:17–18 NLT

God, thank You for the transformative power of Your love. Let it infiltrate my life so I am able to live without stress and fear right now, as well as on judgement day. Your perfect love allows me to be free in every way! Amen.

prayer requests

praises

READ JAMES 4:1–10

You desire but do not have, so you kill. You covet but you cannot get what you want, so you quarrel and fight. You do not have because you do not ask God. When you ask, you do not receive, because you ask with wrong motives, that you may spend what you get on your pleasures.

JAMES 4:2–3 NIV

Father, examine my heart and reveal my inner motives and desires with Your light so that I can seek what is best for You, for myself, and for others. Help me to see the ways my heart can become divided, and may I become a person of peace, able to release my own desires to You. Amen.

prayer requests

praises

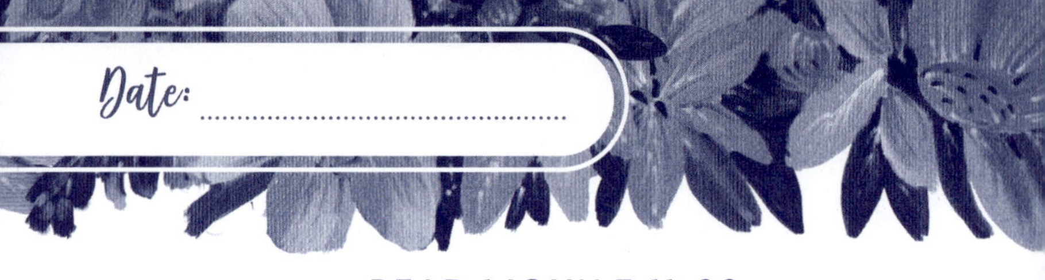

READ 1 JOHN 3:11–20

Dear children, let's not merely say that we love each other; let us show the truth by our actions. Our actions will show that we belong to the truth, so we will be confident when we stand before God.

1 John 3:18–19 NLT

Jesus, when I feel self-conscious and ill-equipped to show love in action, remind me of Your astounding act of humility on the cross. You showed me how to love perfectly, and I want to follow Your example. Put opportunities to love in my path today, Lord. My heart is open, and my hands are ready to do Your will. Amen.

prayer requests

praises

READ PSALM 33:16–22

Don't count on your warhorse to give you victory—for all its strength, it cannot save you. But the LORD watches over those who fear him, those who rely on his unfailing love.

PSALM 33:17–18 NLT

Thank You for watching over me, Father. You keep me safe and preserve my life in ways that I won't know this side of heaven. Your strength is what I put my trust in—not my own, not other people's. I am imperfect, and others will let me down whether they mean to or not. Your redeeming love lifts me up and holds me steady even in hard times. Amen.

prayer requests

praises

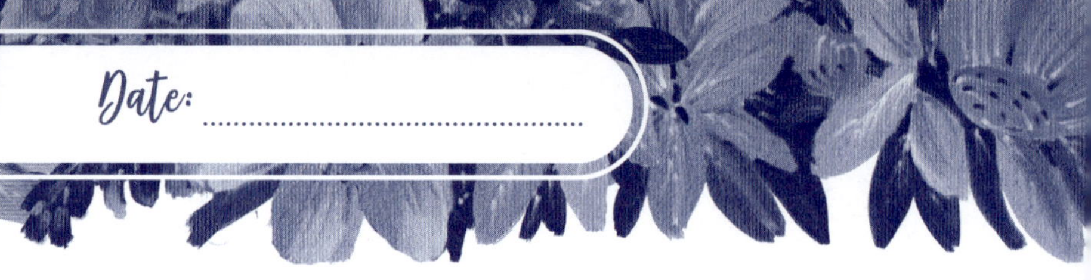

Date: ....

READ ROMANS 5:1–11

For if while we were enemies we were reconciled to God through the death of His Son, much more, having been reconciled, we shall be saved by His life. And not only this, but we also celebrate in God through our Lord Jesus Christ, through whom we have now received the reconciliation.

Romans 5:10–11 nasb

Jesus, thank You for Your love, mercy, and kindness, which You put on display in Your life, death, and resurrection here on earth. I am grateful to be healed, restored, and forgiven for my sins, grateful that I can trust in You without fear or reservation. May I fully live in the love You have poured out in my heart through Your Holy Spirit. Amen.

prayer requests

praises

READ 1 KINGS 8:25–32

"May you watch over this Temple night and day, this place where you have said, 'My name will be there.' May you always hear the prayers I make toward this place. May you hear the humble and earnest requests from me and your people Israel when we pray toward this place. Yes, hear us from heaven where you live, and when you hear, forgive."

1 Kings 8:29–30 NLT

Father, You know that I may struggle and fail today, but I will trust in Your mercy and kindness and rely on the promises You have given me in Jesus. May I remain humble as I seek Your forgiveness and restoration. Amen.

prayer requests

praises

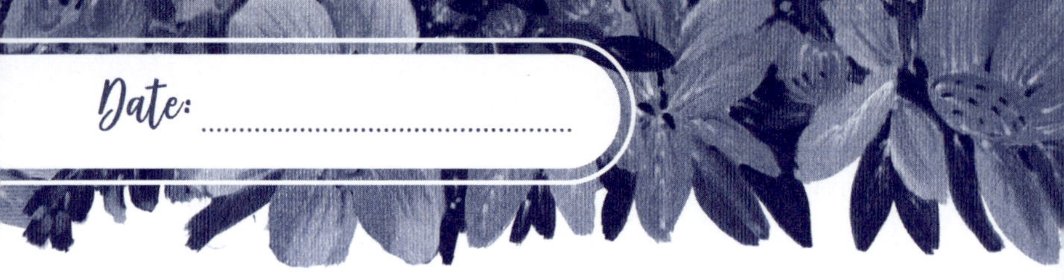

Date: ....

READ PROVERBS 4

Above all else, guard your heart,
for everything you do flows from it.
PROVERBS 4:23 NIV

Holy Spirit, come alive in my heart now. Help me to feel Your presence as I start my day. Turn my heart toward the things that are important to the Father, and guard against the people and situations that can lead to heartsickness. Create in me a pure heart concerned with God's glory. Amen.

prayer requests

praises

READ GENESIS 50:15–21

But Joseph said to them, "Do not be afraid, for am I in God's place? As for you, you meant evil against me, but God meant it for good in order to bring about this present result, to keep many people alive."

GENESIS 50:19–20 NASB

Father, may I always remember the grace and mercy You have shown to me so that I will never hold grudges against others or set myself as a judge over them. May I see Your power at work in my life and respond with faith and hope when challenges surface. Amen.

prayer requests

praises

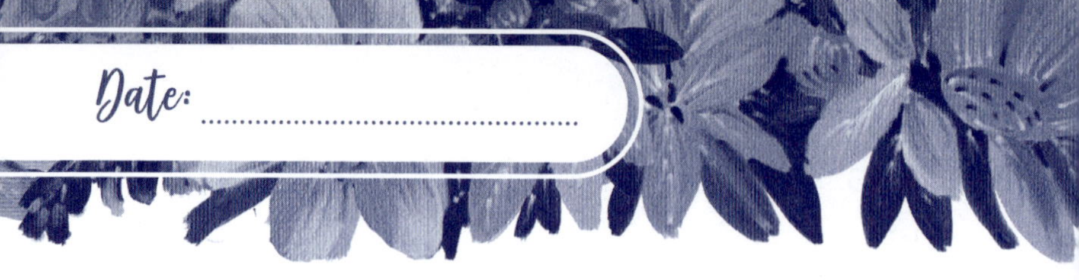

Date: ....

READ ROMANS 12:14–21

Bless those who persecute you. Don't curse them; pray that God will bless them. Be happy with those who are happy, and weep with those who weep.

Romans 12:14–15 NLT

Jesus, help me to see all people as made in Your image and to treat opponents and enemies with compassion and consideration. I surrender my fears and distrust of others to You so that I can serve them and treat them with the same kindness I would hope to receive for myself. Amen.

prayer requests

praises

READ 1 JOHN 4:16–21

There is no fear in love, but perfect love drives out fear, because fear involves punishment, and the one who fears is not perfected in love. We love, because He first loved us.

1 John 4:18–19 NASB

Father, help me to see with clarity the love that You have so generously shown me. May I live free from fear and approach You in prayer with confidence that Your love has come to me before I could do anything for You in return. May I show Your perfect love to those I meet today. Amen.

prayer requests

praises

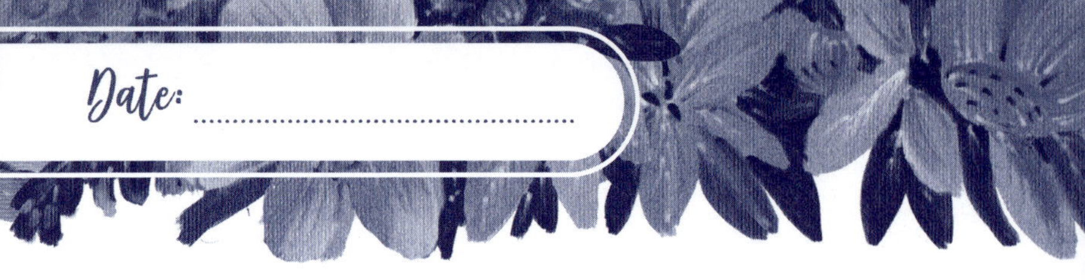

READ ROMANS 8:1–8

So letting your sinful nature control your mind leads to death. But letting the Spirit control your mind leads to life and peace.

Romans 8:6 NLT

God, I'm done giving my sinful nature control of my mind. Today I choose to surrender my thoughts and feelings to Your will. I invite the Holy Spirit to take the helm of my mind. I know with You in control, I will live a peaceful life filled with Your promises. Amen.

prayer requests

praises

READ 2 CORINTHIANS 13:3–10

For to be sure, he was crucified in weakness, yet he lives by God's power. Likewise, we are weak in him, yet by God's power we will live with him in our dealing with you.

2 Corinthians 13:4 niv

Almighty God, sometimes life feels like an unending struggle. I know my own efforts are futile, and I know these challenges aren't me—they're just things that are happening to me. Today I'm asking You to step in with Your power. Cover me, Father, and I know You will take care of it all. Amen.

prayer requests

praises

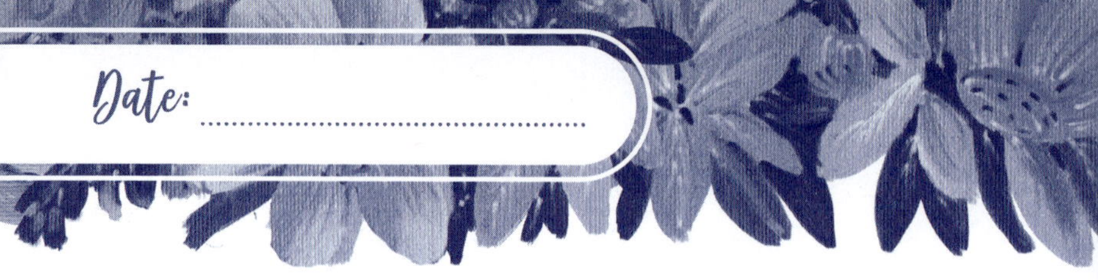

READ DEUTERONOMY 4:9–14

"Assemble the people for me, and I will let them hear my words, so that they may learn to fear me as long as they live on the earth, and may teach their children so."

DEUTERONOMY 4:10 NRSV

Father, help me to notice what is most important and to remember what You have passed along to me both in my spiritual experiences with You and in my knowledge of Your Word. May I invest in the spiritual health of future generations so that they will never forget how You have revealed Yourself. Amen.

prayer requests

praises

READ PSALM 84:5–12

A day in Your courtyards is better than a thousand elsewhere.
I would rather stand at the threshold of the house of my God
than live in the tents of wickedness. For the LORD God is a
sun and shield; the LORD gives grace and glory; He withholds
no good thing from those who walk with integrity.

PSALM 84:10–11 NASB

Father, thank You for the promise to care for the needs of those who walk with integrity and seek You first by dwelling in Your house. May I find what I need in You and forever leave behind the empty promises found among those who seek only their own satisfaction. Amen.

prayer requests

praises

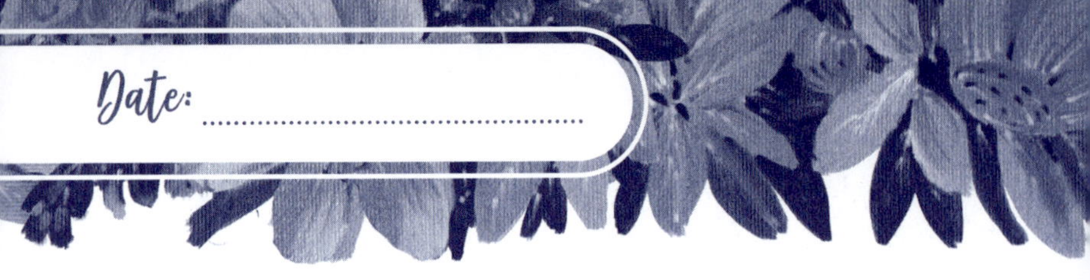
Date:

READ JAMES 3:1–12

For if we could control our tongues, we would be perfect and could also control ourselves in every other way.

James 3:2 NLT

Father, only You can help me get a handle on this powerful muscle in my mouth. My tongue gets me into trouble too often, but I also admit that I too often react with my tongue. Give me the wisdom to know when and what to speak and when to remain silent. Amen.

prayer requests

praises

READ 1 JOHN 3:1–10

See how very much our Father loves us, for he calls us his children, and that is what we are!

1 John 3:1 NLT

When my life, my roles, and my relationships are in flux, Father, remind me who I am. I am Yours. I am a daughter of the King. I am claimed by Jesus as a sister. I am a vital part of the Body of Christ. I am forgiven, cherished, loved, and encouraged in You. Your identity is what I need. When people see me, let me fade into the background, and may Your light shine! Amen.

prayer requests

praises

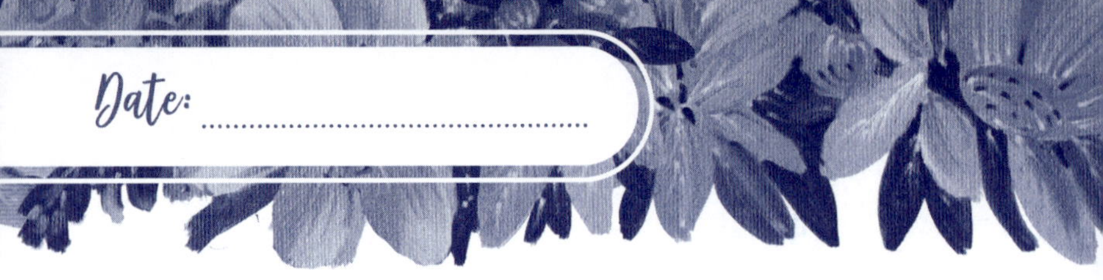

READ 2 CORINTHIANS 4:11–18

For our present troubles are small and won't last very long. Yet they produce for us a glory that vastly outweighs them and will last forever!

2 Corinthians 4:17 nlt

Father, thank You for Your generous comfort and hope that can carry me through the difficulties of today. May I never become so preoccupied with the things of the present moment that I can't see how You've prepared a place for me that will overshadow the pain of today. Amen.

prayer requests

praises

READ JOSHUA 24:14–27

"As for me and my household, we will serve the LORD."

JOSHUA 24:15 NRSV

Father, thank You for the grace and patience You've shown me, and thank You for the spiritual leaders who have helped set a path ahead of me. May I serve You with an undivided heart by choosing to make You my focus for today, tomorrow, and the days that follow. Amen.

prayer requests

praises

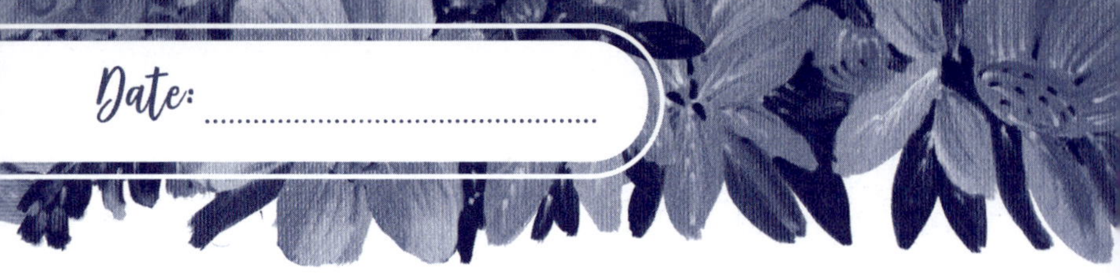

READ EPHESIANS 4:25–32

"Don't sin by letting anger control you." Don't let the sun go down while you are still angry.

Ephesians 4:26 NLT

Jesus, sometimes giving in to anger in the moment just feels good. But I also know the destruction in the wake of an angry outburst is hard to clean up. I've hurt people I love in the past, and that's the last thing I want to do in the future. Give me wisdom to stop and think before reacting in anger today. Amen.

prayer requests

praises

READ PSALM 136

Give thanks to the God of heaven. His love endures forever.

Psalm 136:26 niv

Unending God, I see Your care for me everywhere. From the beauty of Your creation and the blessings You so generously lavish on me, to the people You have placed in my life and the unique talents You have made in me, I feel Your love with every breath I take. Thank You for choosing me. Thank You for loving me always and forever. Amen.

prayer requests

praises

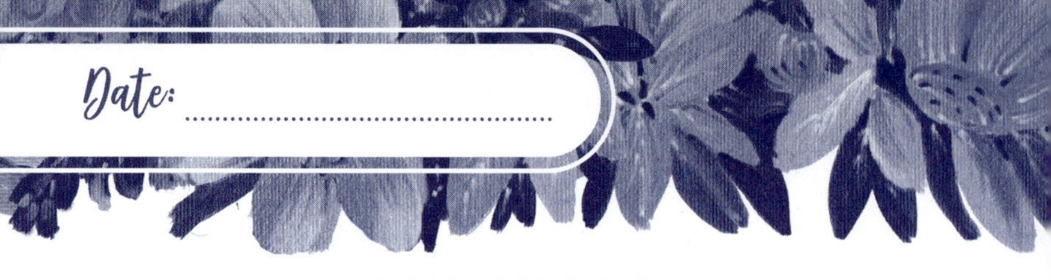

Date: ....

READ ACTS 4:8–14

When they saw the courage of Peter and John and realized that they were unschooled, ordinary men, they were astonished and they took note that these men had been with Jesus. But since they could see the man who had been healed standing there with them, there was nothing they could say.

Acts 4:13–14 niv

Jesus, help me to slow down and to take notice of You throughout my day. I ask for Your wisdom and power so that I can see those in need around me and then intervene for their benefit. May I always do what is right through the courage You provide. Amen.

prayer requests

praises

READ PSALM 105:1–7

Give thanks to the Lord, call upon His name; make His deeds known among the peoples. Sing to Him, sing praises to Him; tell of all His wonders. Boast in His holy name; may the heart of those who seek the Lord be joyful. Seek the Lord and His strength; seek His face continually.

Psalm 105:1–4 NASB

Thank You, Father, for revealing Yourself to me this day and for being present in these quiet moments of study and prayer before You. Help me to recognize the many ways You've blessed me, and help me to take delight in boasting of Your goodness before others. Amen.

prayer requests

praises

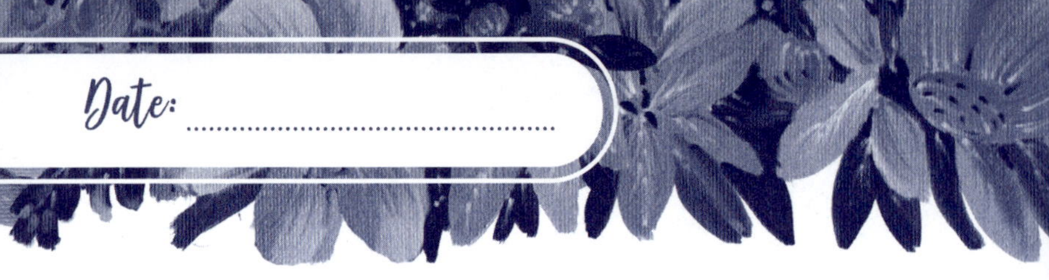

READ 2 CORINTHIANS 5:11–21

Therefore, if anyone is in Christ, he is a new creation.
The old has passed away; behold, the new has come.
2 CORINTHIANS 5:17 ESV

Thank You, Lord, for making me new. You did not leave me in my own sinfulness, and You have such abundant life for me to live out as Your loved child. I want to live each day in eager anticipation of new experiences with You. Draw me close, Father. Continue to make me more like You. I long for continued transformation! Amen.

prayer requests

praises

READ HEBREWS 13:6–19

So we say with confidence, "The Lord is my helper; I will not be afraid. What can mere mortals do to me?"

Hebrews 13:6 niv

Father, I need Your help. I trust You, but fear keeps trying to force its way into my heart and mind. I can't shake these feelings of uncertainty. My brain keeps fretting over scenarios that I know will probably never happen, but I can't stop the thoughts by myself. Fill me with Your peace. Give me the confidence that You are in control and You want the best for me. Amen.

prayer requests

praises

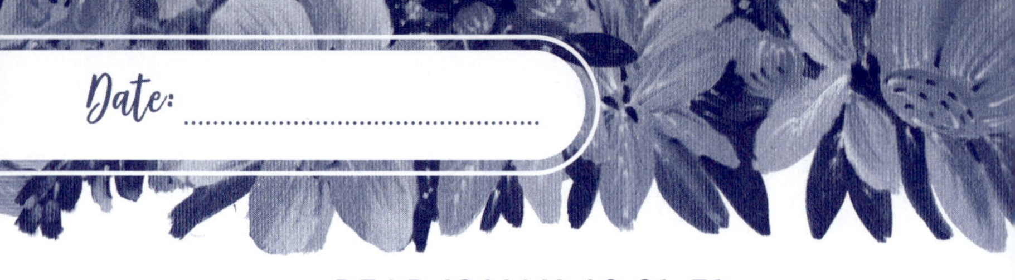

Date: ....

READ ISAIAH 40:21–31

Do you not know? Have you not heard? The Lord is the everlasting God, the Creator of the ends of the earth. He will not grow tired or weary, and his understanding no one can fathom. He gives strength to the weary and increases the power of the weak. Even youths grow tired and weary, and young men stumble and fall; but those who hope in the Lord will renew their strength.

Isaiah 40:28–31 niv

I praise You, Lord, for being mighty and all-powerful. You have created all things on earth, and nothing is outside Your influence. I ask for Your mercy and healing in the places of suffering and grief in my life and in the lives of those around me. May I find hope in Your everlasting promises and renewal in Your loving presence. Amen.

prayer requests

praises

Date:

READ MATTHEW 26:47–56

Then Jesus said to him, "Put your sword back into its place; for all who take the sword will perish by the sword. Do you think that I cannot appeal to my Father, and he will at once send me more than twelve legions of angels?"

MATTHEW 26:52–53 NRSV

Jesus, thank You for Your power and patience, both of which guide our world and give many an opportunity to know You personally. May I imitate Your mercy and restraint with others while also trusting in Your all-powerful rule over the earth. Amen.

prayer requests

praises

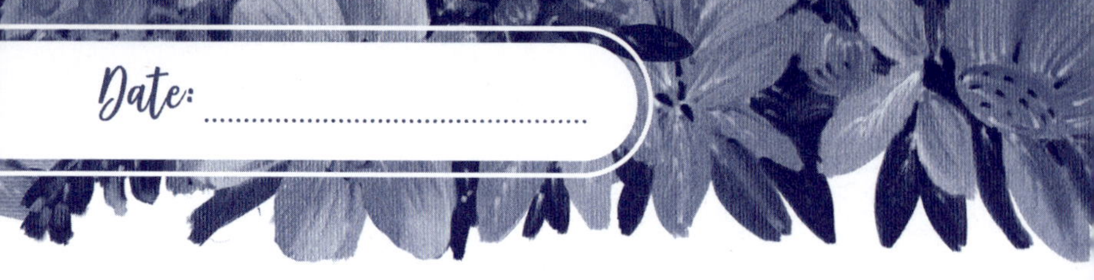

READ EPHESIANS 6:10–20

Therefore put on the full armor of God, so that when the day of evil comes, you may be able to stand your ground, and after you have done everything, to stand.

Ephesians 6:13 NIV

Almighty God, I am not a fierce warrior, but Your Spirit makes me strong. When Satan charges at me, give me Your fearless bravery and the security to know that the power of Your Holy Spirit inside me has already prevailed over every kind of evil. I trust You, Father. Amen.

prayer requests

praises

READ PSALM 40

He lifted me out of the pit of despair, out of the mud and the mire. He set my feet on solid ground and steadied me as I walked along.

Psalm 40:2 NLT

God, thank You for rescuing me. For pulling me out, cleaning me up, and giving me the confidence to walk ahead. Stay with me and keep me from stumbling or jumping head-first into another pit of my own making. Amen.

prayer requests

praises

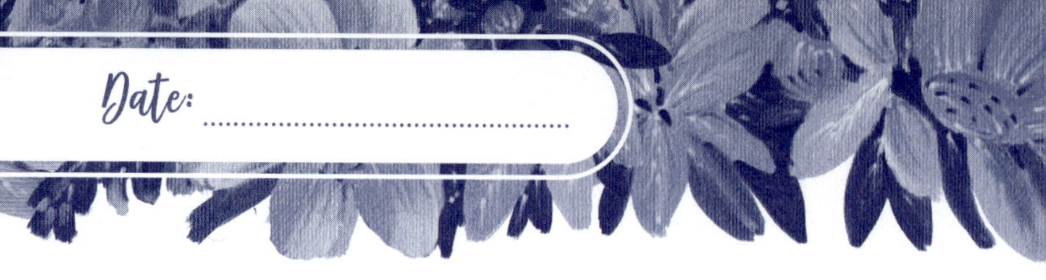

READ PSALM 33:13–22

A horse is a false hope for victory; nor does it rescue anyone by its great strength. Behold, the eye of the LORD is on those who fear Him, on those who wait for His faithfulness.

PSALM 33:17–18 NASB

Thank You, Lord, for Your deep love and concern for Your people. You hear my cries when I call out to You, and You promise to care for me in difficult times. May I leave behind my hope in anything else that promises security and learn to wait patiently for Your help. Amen.

prayer requests

praises

READ GENESIS 39:10–23

But the LORD was with Joseph in the prison and showed him his faithful love. And the LORD made Joseph a favorite with the prison warden. Before long, the warden put Joseph in charge of all the other prisoners and over everything that happened in the prison.

GENESIS 39:21–22 NLT

Lord, thank You for the many models of Your faithfulness and love to those who have suffered unfairly. May I seek You in faith and hope without demanding specific outcomes as the sure sign of Your blessing. May I see each challenge as an opportunity to be shaped and formed into Your servant who is ready to serve others. Amen.

prayer requests

praises

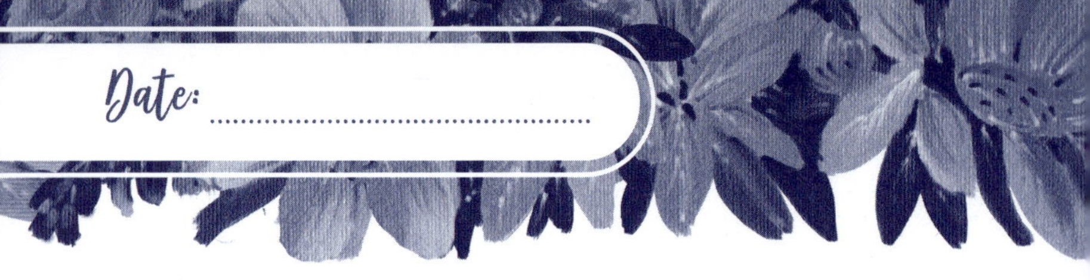

READ PSALM 73

But as for me, it is good to be near God. I have made the Sovereign LORD my refuge; I will tell of all your deeds.

PSALM 73:28 NIV

God, I am here with You, and You are here with me. Make Your presence so real that I cannot deny that I am by Your side. Please give me a glimpse into Your plan, especially when I see situations that I simply do not understand. I long to understand what You are doing behind the scenes. I trust You, Father. Amen.

prayer requests

praises

READ 1 CORINTHIANS 13

When I was a child, I spoke and thought and reasoned as a child. But when I grew up, I put away childish things. Now we see things imperfectly, like puzzling reflections in a mirror, but then we will see everything with perfect clarity. All that I know now is partial and incomplete, but then I will know everything completely, just as God now knows me completely.

1 Corinthians 13:11–12 NLT

Father, thank You for the ability to learn, grow, and mature in my understanding and in my faith in You. Even though I can't understand everything this side of heaven, I want to keep gaining new insight into Your heart, Your desires, and Your plan for me. Amen.

prayer requests

praises

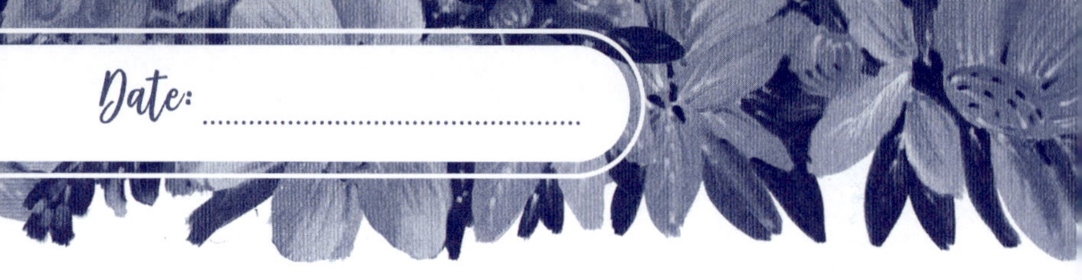

Date: ....

READ ZECHARIAH 1:1–6

"Therefore tell the people: This is what the LORD Almighty says: 'Return to me,' declares the LORD Almighty, 'and I will return to you,' says the LORD Almighty. Do not be like your ancestors, to whom the earlier prophets proclaimed: This is what the LORD Almighty says: 'Turn from your evil ways and your evil practices.' But they would not listen or pay attention to me, declares the LORD."

ZECHARIAH 1:3–4 NIV

Thank You, Lord, that Your mercy and forgiveness overcome my greatest failures and deepest shame. Help me to learn from the mistakes of past generations who rejected Your mercy. May I make a definitive choice to return to You with an open heart and a teachable mind. Amen.

prayer requests

praises

READ EXODUS 15:1–11

Then Moses and the Israelites sang this song to the LORD: "I will sing to the LORD, for he is highly exalted. Both horse and driver he has hurled into the sea. "The LORD is my strength and my defense; he has become my salvation. He is my God, and I will praise him, my father's God, and I will exalt him."

EXODUS 15:1–2 NIV

Thank You, Lord, for the ways You have provided and cared for Your people throughout the years. . .and for the ways You have provided and cared for me. Today I will remember and rejoice in Your provision and kindness toward me, trusting that You will never fail me. Amen.

prayer requests

praises

READ JOHN 14:15–26

"And I will ask the Father, and he will give you another Helper, to be with you forever, even the Spirit of truth, whom the world cannot receive, because it neither sees him nor knows him. You know him, for he dwells with you and will be in you."

JOHN 14:16–17 ESV

Spirit of God, sometimes You are a mystery to me. But I long to know You better. Come alive in my heart today and make Your presence known. Jesus said You are my helper. So, I am asking for Your help. Help me even when I act like I don't need it. Amen.

prayer requests

praises

READ PHILIPPIANS 3:7–21

I do not say that I have received this or have already become perfect. But I keep going on to make that life my own as Christ Jesus made me His own. . . . My eyes are on the crown. I want to win the race and get the crown of God's call from heaven through Christ Jesus.

PHILIPPIANS 3:12, 14 NLV

God, I am ready for this challenge. This is a race that fills me with joy, and I want to run with excellence. Pick me up when I stumble and set me on solid footing so I will run again. Amen.

prayer requests

praises

READ 1 KINGS 11:1–13

In Solomon's old age, they turned his heart to worship other gods instead of being completely faithful to the LORD his God, as his father, David, had been. Solomon worshiped Ashtoreth, the goddess of the Sidonians, and Molech, the detestable god of the Ammonites.

1 KINGS 11:4–5 NLT

Thank You, Lord, for Your mercy and forgiveness that lift me up whenever I fail. Please examine my heart and expose any places that are divided or not given wholly to You so that I can serve You and Your people with a single-minded commitment all the days of my life. Amen.

prayer requests

praises

Date: ....

READ PSALM 102:12–22

For the Lord will build up Zion; he will appear in his glory.
He will regard the prayer of the destitute, and will not despise
their prayer. Let this be recorded for a generation to come,
so that a people yet unborn may praise the Lord.

Psalm 102:16–18 NRSV

Lord, You see my suffering and the suffering of others, and You desire to bring justice and relief to all who suffer. Help me to wait patiently for You, placing my faith in Your everlasting power and the hope that You will one day return to earth to rule. Amen.

prayer requests

praises

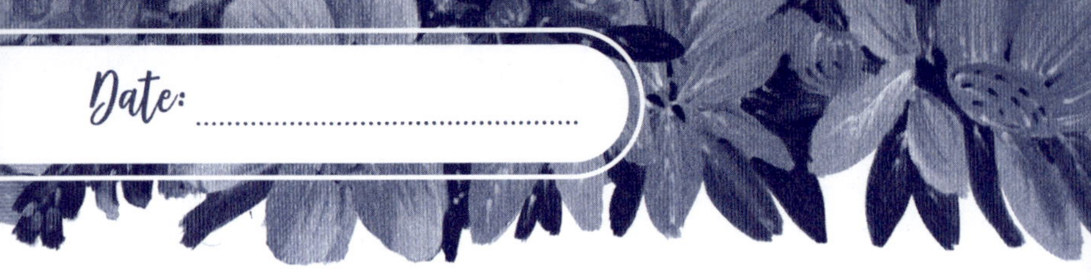

READ JOHN 14:27–31

"Peace I leave with you. My peace I give to you."

John 14:27 NLV

Savior, Your peace is what I long for. Fill me with the deep restfulness and contentment that only You can offer. When I try to take back control, gently remind me that the only way to peace is to let it go. Make me an instrument of Your peace to everyone around me today and energize me as I walk the path You lay before me. Amen.

prayer requests

praises

Date: ....

READ ROMANS 8:9–17

The Spirit of God, who raised Jesus from the dead, lives in you.

Romans 8:11 NLT

Spirit of God, move mightily in me. I am humbled and honored when I realize it was Your power that brought Jesus back to life. It was Your power that conquered death once and for all. And it is Your power that makes my salvation possible. All of that is enough, but You are my helper and guide. Please make me bold, fearless, confident, and powerful in the name of Jesus Christ to do big things for the Father's glory. Amen.

prayer requests

praises

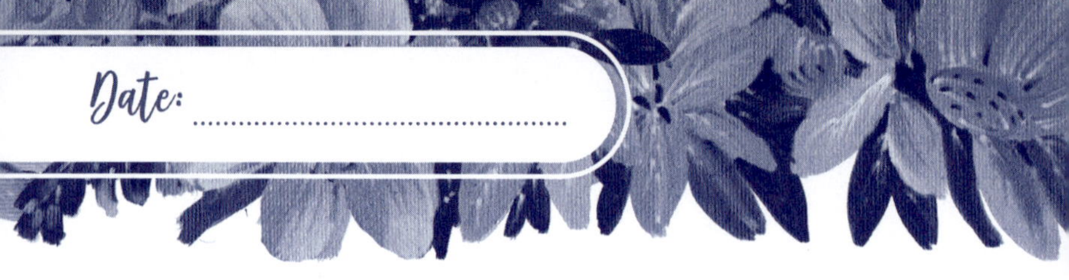

READ MATTHEW 5:1–11

"Blessed are the meek, for they will inherit the earth. Blessed are those who hunger and thirst for righteousness, for they will be filled. Blessed are the merciful, for they will be shown mercy. Blessed are the pure in heart, for they will see God."

MATTHEW 5:5–8 NIV

Jesus, help me to see the world through Your eyes and to value what You value. May I look ahead to the rewards You have promised me, and may I take actions that bring benefit to those around me. I ask that Your power and influence in my life would lead me to a pure heart and a greater awareness of You. Amen.

prayer requests

praises

READ DEUTERONOMY 11:1–12

Observe therefore all the commands I am giving you today, so that you may have the strength to go in and take over the land that you are crossing the Jordan to possess, and so that you may live long in the land the Lord *swore to your ancestors to give to them and their descendants, a land flowing with milk and honey.*

Deuteronomy 11:8–9 niv

Thank You, Lord, for the ways You've been present for Your people, providing for their needs and delivering them from trouble. May I live today with an awareness of Your power and ability to save. And may my awareness of You help me to live in faithful obedience. Amen.

prayer requests

praises

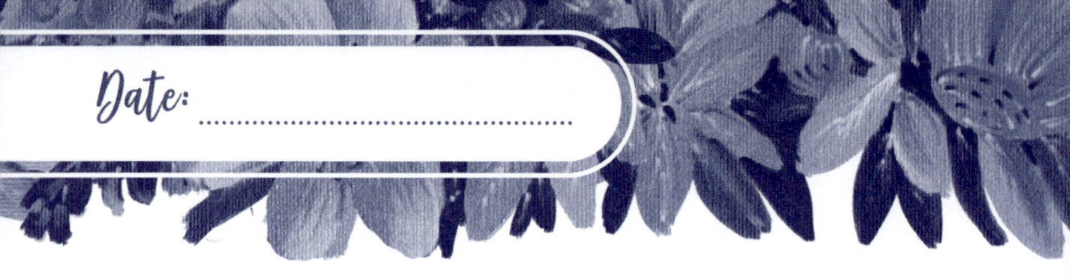

Date:

READ PHILIPPIANS 2:12–18

Do all things without grumbling or disputing, that you may be blameless and innocent, children of God without blemish in the midst of a crooked and twisted generation, among whom you shine as lights in the world.

PHILIPPIANS 2:14–16 ESV

God, I'm guilty of whining when I should be praising You for Your endless goodness to me. Forgive me. I want to be Your blameless and innocent daughter who can point others to Your love. Take away any discontentment and bitterness in my heart and replace it with Your joy. Amen.

prayer requests

praises

READ PROVERBS 4:18–27

Look straight ahead, and fix your eyes on what lies before you.
Mark out a straight path for your feet; stay on the safe path.
Don't get sidetracked; keep your feet from following evil.

PROVERBS 4:25–27 NLT

Father, I admit that I am prone to wander, prone to distractions, prone to getting sidetracked. Forgive me when my eyes veer from You. Shine Your light on the safe path and nudge me back onto the straight way when necessary. I am following You and only You with my whole heart, soul, mind, and strength. Thank You for being a perfect leader. Amen.

prayer requests

praises

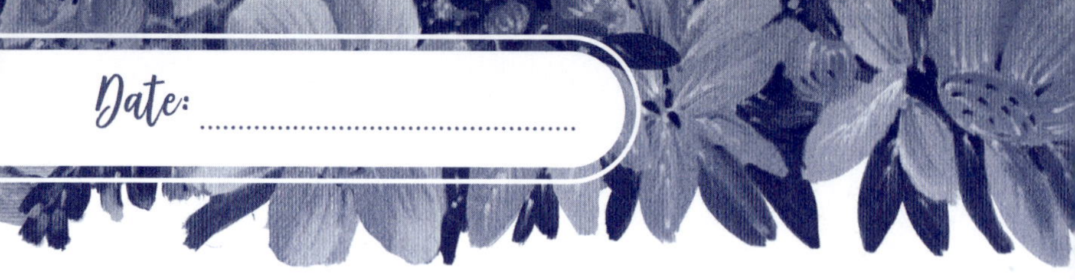

READ 1 SAMUEL 23:13–24

Jonathan went to find David and encouraged him to stay strong in his faith in God. "Don't be afraid," Jonathan reassured him. "My father will never find you! You are going to be the king of Israel, and I will be next to you, as my father, Saul, is well aware."

1 Samuel 23:16–17 NLT

Help me, Lord, to see the people around me who are discouraged, struggling with their faith, or facing adversity and uncertainty. May I support them with encouragement and intercession when they are most in need of compassionate, considerate help. Amen.

prayer requests

praises

READ 2 CHRONICLES 32:1–8

"Be strong and courageous, do not fear or be dismayed because of the king of Assyria nor because of all the horde that is with him; for the One with us is greater than the one with him. With him is only an arm of flesh, but with us is the LORD our God to help us and to fight our battles." And the people relied on the words of Hezekiah king of Judah.

2 CHRONICLES 32:7–8 NASB

Lord, You know better than I do what my challenges are and how I can best overcome them. Thank You for being near Your people in their times of challenge and struggle. May Your power work on my behalf so that I am safe in Your presence. Amen.

prayer requests

praises

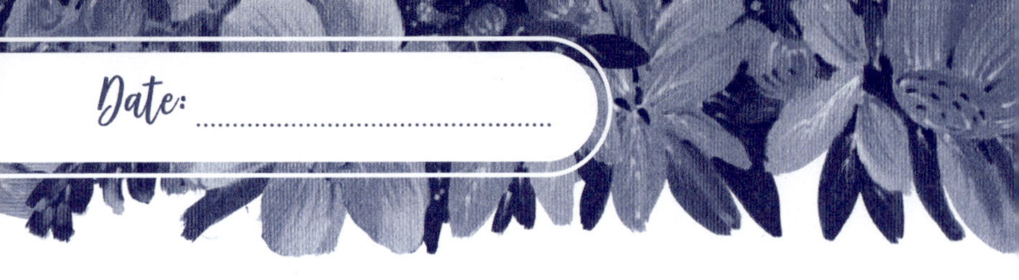

Date: ....

READ 1 CORINTHIANS 12:12–26

So God has put the body together such that extra honor and care are given to those parts that have less dignity. This makes for harmony among the members, so that all the members care for each other. If one part suffers, all the parts suffer with it, and if one part is honored, all the parts are glad.

1 Corinthians 12:24–26 NLT

Jesus, I am thankful for my church. We are Your body, made up of flawed individuals, but You bind us together in unity, and we are better for it. Forgive me when I wrongly believe I am better on my own. Amen.

prayer requests

praises

READ PROVERBS 17:13–28

A joyful heart is good medicine, but a crushed spirit dries up the bones.

PROVERBS 17:22 ESV

Joyful Father, I am so thankful that You are a God who delights in laughter. You invite me to unburden my spirit (Psalm 55:22), and joy comes rushing in. Show me how to cultivate a heart bursting with Your hope and joy so I can share it with others. Give me pockets of laughter throughout my day. May it be Your soothing cure to my parched spirit and good medicine for everyone around me. Amen.

prayer requests

praises

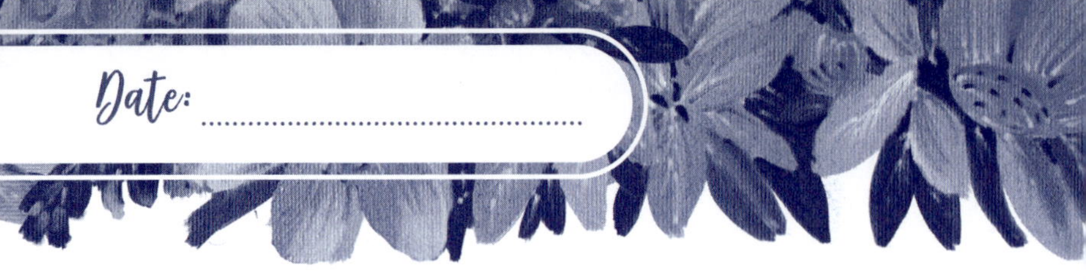

Date:

READ PSALM 5:1–8

But I, through the abundance of your steadfast love,
will enter your house, I will bow down toward your holy
temple in awe of you. Lead me, O Lord, in your righteousness
because of my enemies; make your way straight before me.
Psalm 5:7–8 NRSV

Thank You, Lord, for Your love, grace, and mercy—all of which You promise will meet me in my weakness and uncertainty today. May I find the time in my day to share my requests with You and then trust that You will guide me in the correct path forward. Amen.

prayer requests

praises

READ LUKE 5:27–39

But the Pharisees and the teachers of the law who belonged to their sect complained to his disciples, "Why do you eat and drink with tax collectors and sinners?" Jesus answered them, "It is not the healthy who need a doctor, but the sick. I have not come to call the righteous, but sinners to repentance."

LUKE 5:30–32 NIV

Thank You, Jesus, for coming to heal me and restore me so that I no longer need to live in shame or struggle to obey You. May I enjoy the liberty and freedom that comes from knowing You, and may I share that healing and hope with those I meet today. Amen.

prayer requests

praises

Date:

READ MATTHEW 6:5–13

"When you pray, do not be as those who pretend to be someone they are not. They love to stand and pray in the places of worship or in the streets so people can see them. . . . When you pray, go into a room by yourself. After you have shut the door, pray to your Father Who is in secret. Then your Father Who sees in secret will reward you."

Matthew 6:5–6 NLV

Father, I come before You this morning with no motive other than to be in Your presence. I am not pretending to be better than I am. I admit that I have no answers. I realize that I can't do life today without You. I need You, God. Please be near and never leave me. Amen.

prayer requests

praises

READ 2 CORINTHIANS 1:12–24

For our boast is this, the testimony of our conscience, that we behaved in the world with simplicity and godly sincerity, not by earthly wisdom but by the grace of God, and supremely so toward you.

2 Corinthians 1:12 ESV

Jesus, I've tried for too long to live the way the world tells me I should. It's exhausting trying to have it all, understand it all, do it all, and look flawless in the process. Give me Your wisdom to know what is essential: love, generosity, truth, forgiveness. Help me to live a life of simplicity and sincerity rooted in You. Amen.

prayer requests

praises

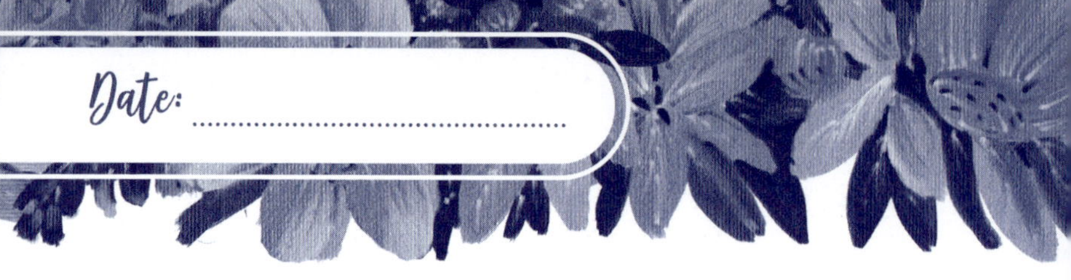

READ 1 PETER 2:11–25

For it is God's will that by doing right you should silence the ignorance of the foolish. As servants of God, live as free people, yet do not use your freedom as a pretext for evil.

1 Peter 2:15–16 NRSV

Thank You, Jesus, that You have set me free to be Your servant, a servant who is free to love others. When I am misunderstood or treated unfairly, help me to remember how You were mistreated and still showed mercy so that I can honor everyone and respond with Your same grace. Amen.

prayer requests

praises

READ 1 KINGS 19:1–9

The angel of the Lord came back a second time and touched him and said, "Get up and eat, for the journey is too much for you." So he got up and ate and drank. Strengthened by that food, he traveled forty days and forty nights until he reached Horeb, the mountain of God.

1 Kings 19:7–8 niv

Thank You, Lord, for Your presence and provision during difficult times. I ask that You lift me up and encourage me in the moments when I feel most overwhelmed and uncertain about what's next. May I find courage and hope in Your comforting presence. Amen.

prayer requests

praises

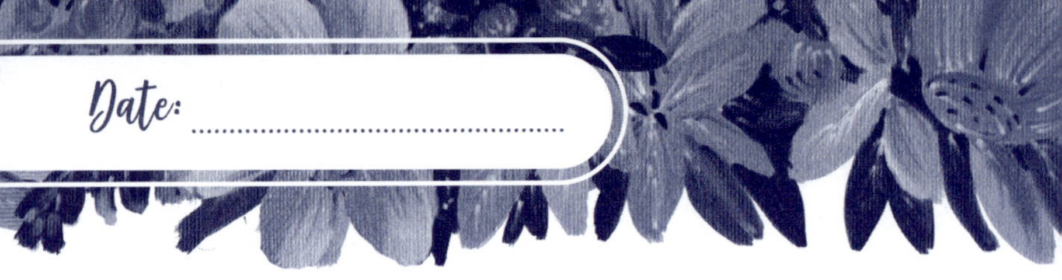

READ PHILIPPIANS 2:1–11

Don't be selfish; don't try to impress others. Be humble, thinking of others as better than yourselves. Don't look out only for your own interests, but take an interest in others, too.

PHILIPPIANS 2:3–4 NLT

Jesus, thank You for showing me the way to humility. When I think I am better than others, remind me of what You did on earth. You lived humbly, with no place to call home. You gave up everything for me. I cannot repay You for that, but I will offer my life as a humble offering to You. Amen.

prayer requests

praises

READ REVELATION 3:14–22

Here I am! I stand at the door and knock. If anyone hears my voice and opens the door, I will come in and eat with that person, and they with me.

REVELATION 3:20 NIV

Father, I'm listening intently for Your knock. When I hear Your voice, I will throw wide the door to my heart to invite You in. Come, eat with me. Let's talk and laugh and cry together. It is my heart's longing to know You more and more. Amen.

prayer requests

praises

READ ISAIAH 61

The Spirit of the Sovereign Lord is upon me, for the Lord has anointed me to bring good news to the poor. He has sent me to comfort the brokenhearted and to proclaim that captives will be released and prisoners will be freed. He has sent me to tell those who mourn that the time of the Lord's favor has come, and with it, the day of God's anger against their enemies.

Isaiah 61:1–2 NLT

Father, thank You for the ways You've guided and empowered Your people throughout history. Lead me forward today and give me ears to hear Your calling so that I can serve those in the greatest need of Your healing touch and hopeful message. Amen.

prayer requests

praises

READ PSALM 27:1–10

One thing I have asked from the LORD, that I shall seek: that I may dwell in the house of the LORD all the days of my life, to behold the beauty of the LORD and to meditate in His temple. For on the day of trouble He will conceal me in His tabernacle; He will hide me in the secret place of His tent; He will lift me up on a rock.

PSALM 27:4–5 NASB

Thank You, Lord, for Your comforting and empowering presence. Help me to remain in You so that I can be full of faith and hope in Your power and guidance. May I stay mindful of Your promise to never leave or forsake me as the difficulties of life increase. Amen.

prayer requests

praises

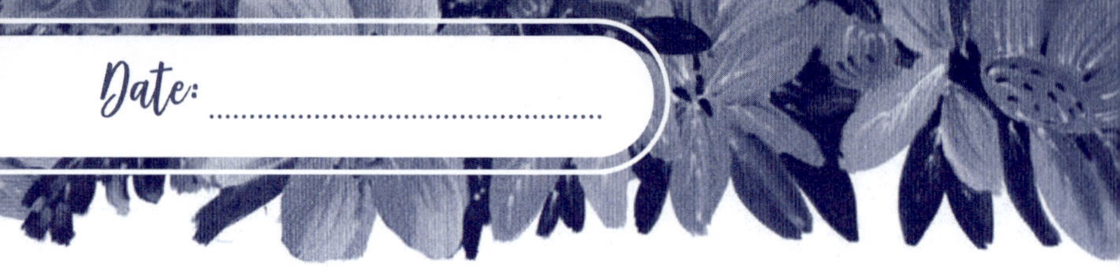

READ ROMANS 6:1–14

For sin shall no longer be your master, because you are not under the law, but under grace.

Romans 6:14 niv

Jesus, I long to be free of the sin that so easily pops up in my life. Old habits are hard to break, but I know that Your power is stronger than any temptation I can face. Help me to live confidently in Your grace, today and every day. And help me to extend that grace to others who have yet to know You. Amen.

prayer requests

praises

READ 1 PETER 3:8–22

Finally, all of you, be like-minded, be sympathetic, love one another, be compassionate and humble. Do not repay evil with evil or insult with insult. On the contrary, repay evil with blessing, because to this you were called so that you may inherit a blessing.

1 Peter 3:8–9 niv

Jesus, Peter is challenging me to take on some of Your very best characteristics in these verses. They sound so unlike me though that I know I can't be this person without Your help. Transform me from the inside out, Jesus. I am called to have sympathy, love, compassion, and humility. Lead me in all of these things, Savior. Amen.

prayer requests

praises

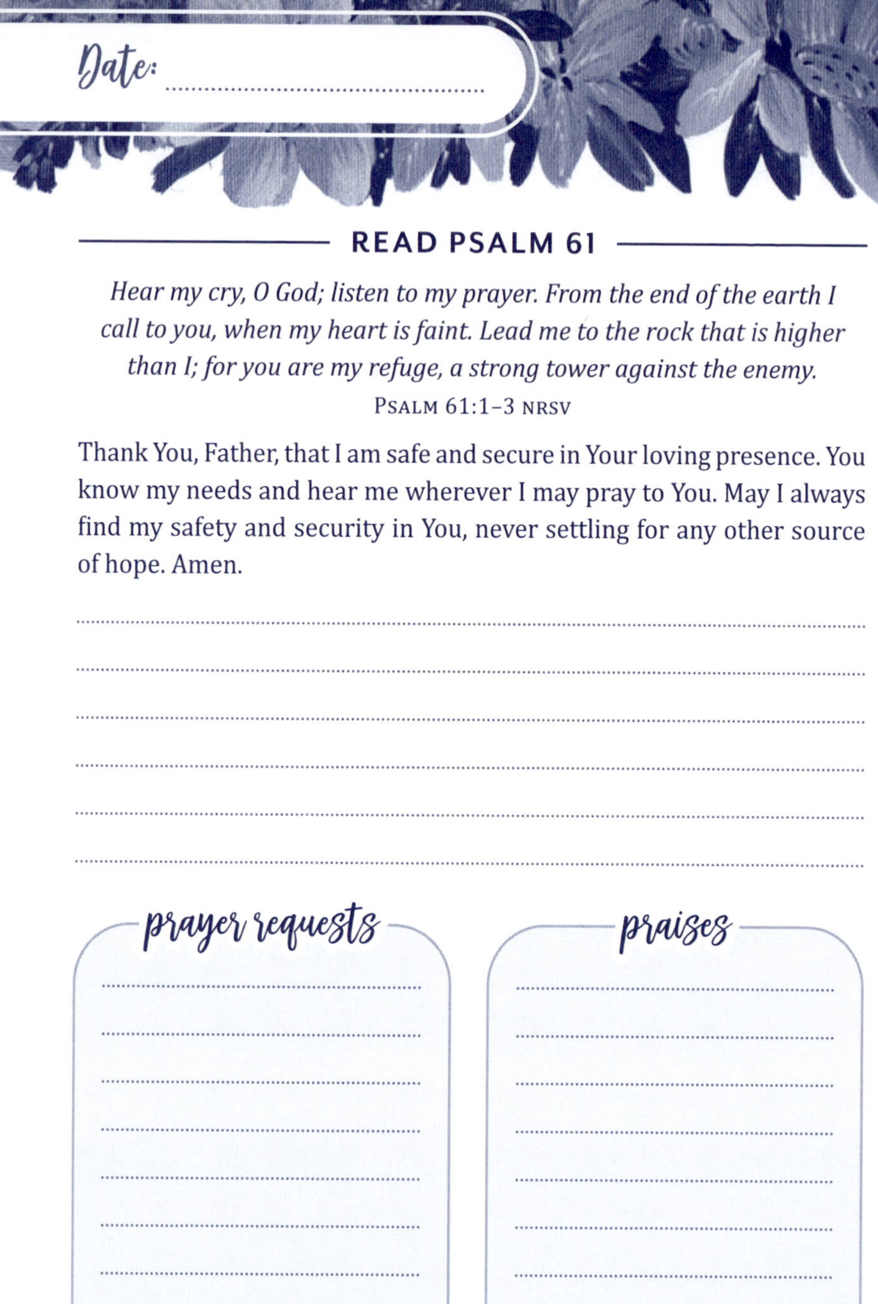

READ PSALM 61

Hear my cry, O God; listen to my prayer. From the end of the earth I call to you, when my heart is faint. Lead me to the rock that is higher than I; for you are my refuge, a strong tower against the enemy.

PSALM 61:1–3 NRSV

Thank You, Father, that I am safe and secure in Your loving presence. You know my needs and hear me wherever I may pray to You. May I always find my safety and security in You, never settling for any other source of hope. Amen.

prayer requests

praises

READ LUKE 15:11–32

" 'But when this son of yours who has squandered your property with prostitutes comes home, you kill the fattened calf for him!' 'My son,' the father said, 'you are always with me, and everything I have is yours. But we had to celebrate and be glad, because this brother of yours was dead and is alive again; he was lost and is found.' "

LUKE 15:30–32 NIV

Thank You, Father, for Your mercy and kindness—for Your promises I can always return to You and celebrate in Your mercy and hope of renewal. May I share Your grace and mercy with others who are also in need of restoration and a new chance to live in obedience to You. Amen.

prayer requests

praises

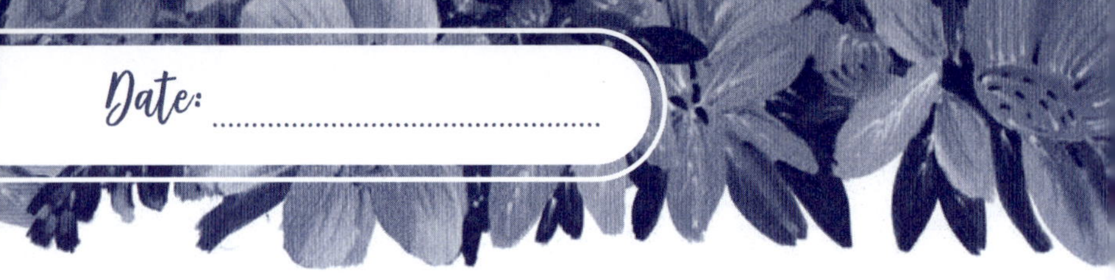

READ 2 CORINTHIANS 9:6–15

You will be enriched in every way so that you can be generous on every occasion, and through us your generosity will result in thanksgiving to God.

2 Corinthians 9:11 niv

Lord God, You are so good to me! I am not taking for granted anything You give to me. I am so blessed! Show me where You want me to be generous today. Keep my motives pure and my eyes open to Your will. My desire is for Your blessings to not stop here but flow through me. Amen.

prayer requests

praises

READ 1 CORINTHIANS 6:12–20

"I have the right to do anything," you say—but not everything is beneficial. "I have the right to do anything"—but I will not be mastered by anything.

1 Corinthians 6:12 niv

Jesus, I'm so thankful that Your work on the cross allows me to live in freedom. I'm not shackled by the requirements of the Old Testament law or any other religion's regulation, and I'm so grateful for that. Give me the wisdom to live wisely in my freedom—to live in a thoughtful, intentional way that honors You. Amen.

prayer requests

praises

READ ISAIAH 53

He was despised and rejected—a man of sorrows, acquainted with deepest grief. We turned our backs on him and looked the other way. He was despised, and we did not care. Yet it was our weaknesses he carried; it was our sorrows that weighed him down.

Isaiah 53:3–4 nlt

Help me, Father, to see my suffering as an opportunity to draw near to You and to remember that You see my sorrow. May I acknowledge my pain and remain aware of those enduring grief and loss so that I can imitate the example of Jesus. Amen.

prayer requests

praises

READ ZECHARIAH 8:1–13

"All this may seem impossible to you now, a small remnant of God's people. But is it impossible for me? says the Lord *of Heaven's Armies. This is what the* Lord *of Heaven's Armies says: You can be sure that I will rescue my people from the east and from the west. I will bring them home again to live safely in Jerusalem. They will be my people, and I will be faithful and just toward them as their God."*

Zechariah 8:6–8 NLT

Help me, Lord, to look at Your character and Your promises with faith and hope so that I can put my complete trust in You today. May I find Your strength to live in obedience and to write a new story of restoration that rights the wrongs of the past. Amen.

prayer requests

praises

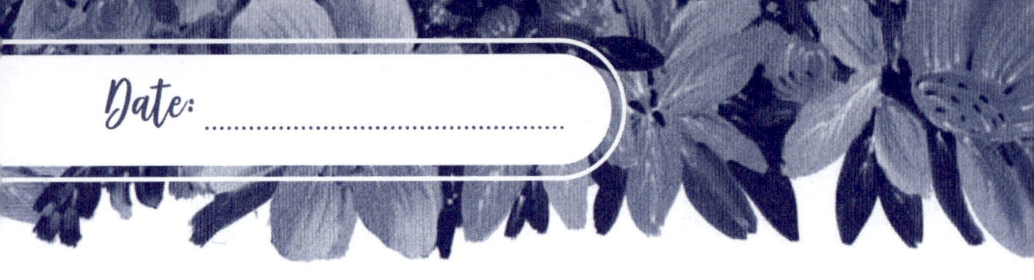

READ JAMES 1:2–18

Count it all joy. . .when you meet trials of various kinds, for you know that the testing of your faith produces steadfastness. And let steadfastness have its full effect, that you may be perfect and complete, lacking in nothing.

James 1:2–4 ESV

Almighty Father, I long to experience Your joy. But it is hard to be joyful when everything is so difficult right now. Help me to look past the challenges of today to see what You're doing in my life and in my current situation. I love You and I trust You. Amen.

prayer requests

praises

READ PROVERBS 15

A gentle answer turns away wrath,
but a harsh word stirs up anger.
Proverbs 15:1 niv

God, I need help controlling the words that come out of my mouth. You know the people and the situations that light me up and make me see red. But I have a choice in my reactions and responses. I want to choose gentleness. I want to bring Your peace into every situation. Show me how, because I can't do it by myself. Amen.

prayer requests

praises

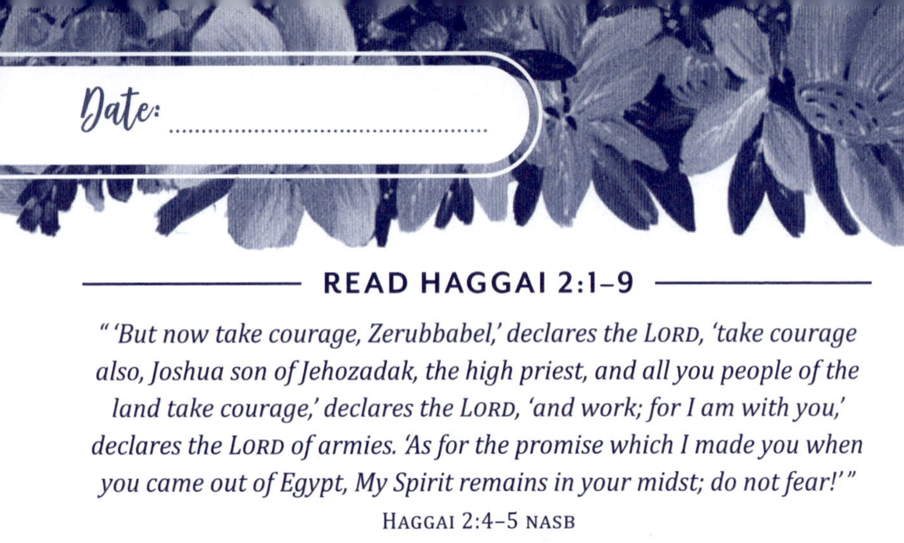

READ HAGGAI 2:1–9

" 'But now take courage, Zerubbabel,' declares the LORD, 'take courage also, Joshua son of Jehozadak, the high priest, and all you people of the land take courage,' declares the LORD, 'and work; for I am with you,' declares the LORD of armies. 'As for the promise which I made you when you came out of Egypt, My Spirit remains in your midst; do not fear!' "

HAGGAI 2:4–5 NASB

Lord, help me to ignore my doubts and the negative thoughts of others so that I can seek You and Your will alone. May I have faith in You to make the courageous choice that rests fully in You and Your faithful Spirit. Amen.

prayer requests

praises

READ PSALM 68:1–10

Father of orphans and protector of widows is God in his holy habitation. God gives the desolate a home to live in; he leads out the prisoners to prosperity, but the rebellious live in a parched land.

Psalm 68:5–6 NRSV

Lord, You are compassionate and kind. Help me to see others the way You see them and to approach You in prayer with confidence and hope. Amen.

prayer requests

praises

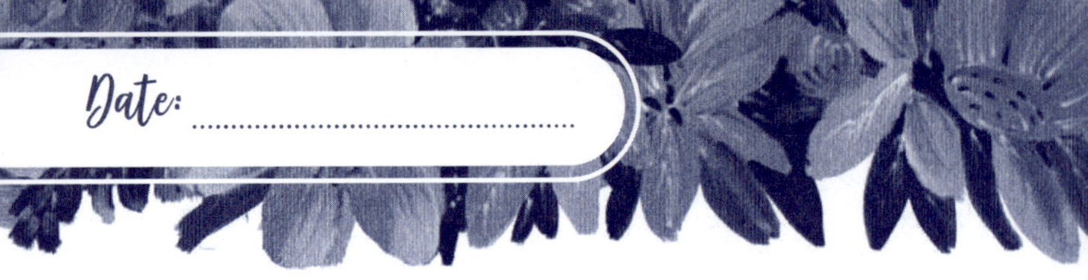

READ COLOSSIANS 3:18–25

Work willingly at whatever you do, as though you were working for the Lord rather than for people.

Colossians 3:23 NLT

Lord God, I give my job to You. I give my role in my family to You. I give every task and responsibility to You. Bless my boss and the other leaders I work with and for. Let me be an encouragement to them and to others around me. I want to be Your light wherever I am. Amen.

prayer requests

praises

READ PSALM 66

But truly God has listened; he has attended to the voice of my prayer. Blessed be God, because he has not rejected my prayer or removed his steadfast love from me!

Psalm 66:19–20 esv

Father, thank You for hearing and listening to my voice when I call to You in prayer. When You listen, I feel loved, accepted, and understood. Today I am listening for You. Speak, Lord, and I will hear and understand. Amen.

prayer requests

praises

Date:

READ LAMENTATIONS 3:19–38

I recall this to my mind, therefore I wait. The LORD's acts of mercy indeed do not end, for His compassions do not fail. They are new every morning; great is Your faithfulness. "The LORD is my portion," says my soul, "therefore I wait for Him."

LAMENTATIONS 3:21–24 NASB

Help me, Lord, to see if I'm relying on anything other than You. May I find peace and rest in the promise of Your mercy and compassion so that I can live with joy and peace as I endure even the most trying moments of my life. Amen.

prayer requests

praises

READ 2 TIMOTHY 2:1–13

Share in suffering like a good soldier of Christ Jesus. No one serving in the army gets entangled in everyday affairs; the soldier's aim is to please the enlisting officer. And in the case of an athlete, no one is crowned without competing according to the rules.

2 Timothy 2:3–5 NRSV

Jesus, help me to compete for the crown of life You offer and to leave all other distractions and misplaced priorities behind. May I become entangled in only Your loving presence and the work that You have set before me today. Amen.

prayer requests

praises

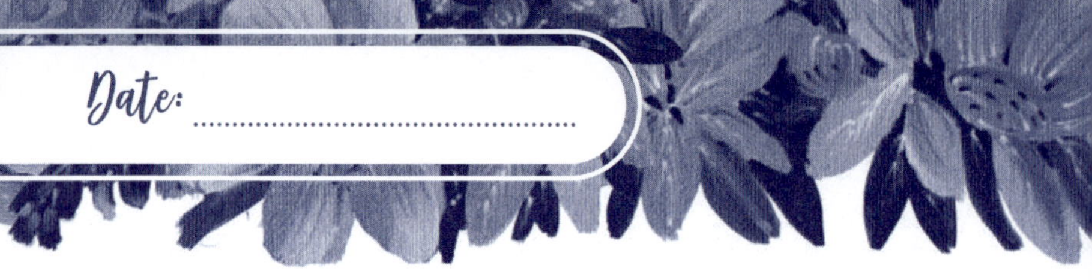

READ EPHESIANS 5:15–20

Make the most of every opportunity in these evil days. Don't act thoughtlessly, but understand what the Lord wants you to do.

Ephesians 5:16–17 NLT

Father, forgive me for wasting Your gift of time. Give me the wisdom to be busy in Your work, moving toward goals that further Your kingdom and draw others closer to You. Make my times of rest holy and refreshing so I can continue to give You my best. Amen.

prayer requests

praises

READ PROVERBS 31:10–31

She opens her mouth with wisdom, and the teaching of kindness is on her tongue.

Proverbs 31:26 esv

God, help me to follow Your example and the example of the Proverbs 31 woman in kindness. Give me the wisdom to understand the difference between kindness and niceness. When the world is fake, make me genuine in my interactions. You are so faithful in Your kindness toward me, and I want to reflect the same to others. Amen.

prayer requests

praises

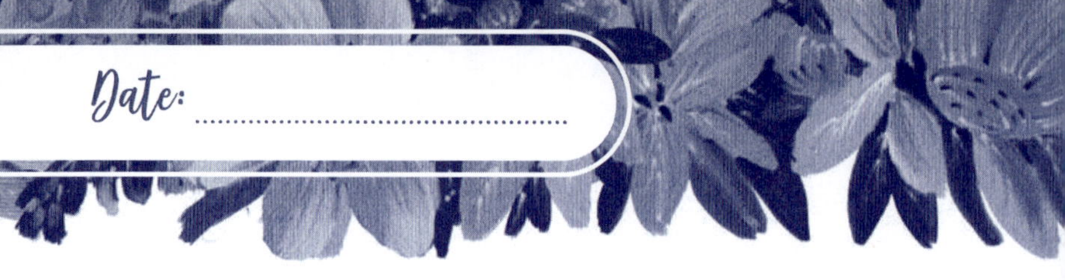

READ 1 SAMUEL 25

David said to Abigail, "Praise be to the LORD, the God of Israel, who has sent you today to meet me. May you be blessed for your good judgment and for keeping me from bloodshed this day and from avenging myself with my own hands.

1 SAMUEL 25:32–33 NIV

Lord, give me the wisdom of Abigail. Help me to be a problem solver for Your Kingdom. Where wisdom is needed, I ask that You grant me a sound mind. When I need to take action, I pray that You will show me that as well. In Jesus' name I ask these things. Amen.

prayer requests

praises

READ NEHEMIAH 4:11–20

When I saw their fear, I stood and said to the nobles, the officials, and the rest of the people: "Do not be afraid of them; remember the Lord who is great and awesome, and fight for your brothers, your sons, your daughters, your wives, and your houses." Now when our enemies heard that it was known to us, and that God had frustrated their plan, then all of us returned to the wall, each one to his work.

NEHEMIAH 4:14–15 NASB

Help me, Lord, to see Your power and love with greater clarity than anything else in my life. May I commit myself to the work You've given to me and never fall away when adversity comes or affliction threatens my perseverance. Amen.

prayer requests

praises

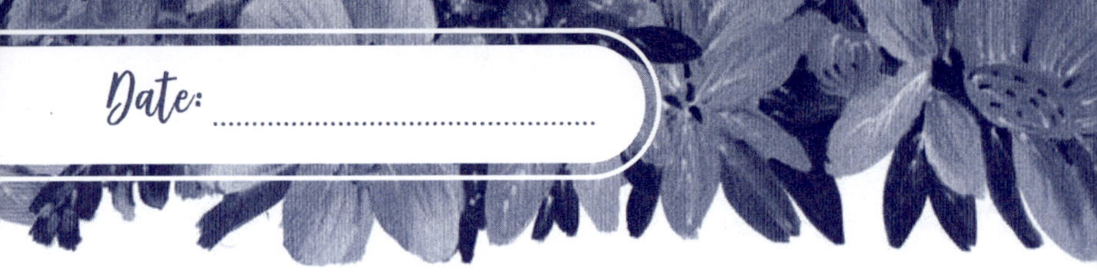

Date:

READ JOHN 8:31–47

"So if the Son sets you free, you will be free indeed."

John 8:36 NIV

Jesus, fill me with Your truth today so that I may live in real freedom. I admit that I too often return to my own filth and selfish desires, and sometimes I start to feel sin's death grip try to take hold again. Forgive me. I am here, standing in the love of our Father as Your sister and friend. Amen.

prayer requests

praises

READ GALATIANS 6:1–10

Do not let yourselves get tired of doing good. If we do not give up, we will get what is coming to us at the right time.

Galatians 6:9 NLV

God, when life gets crazy, I start to develop a bad attitude about the good things You have given me to do. Renew in me a passion for Your work. Give me eyes to see how my efforts play a part in Your plan. And encourage me in my work so I can stay excited and vitalized to do it. Amen.

prayer requests

praises

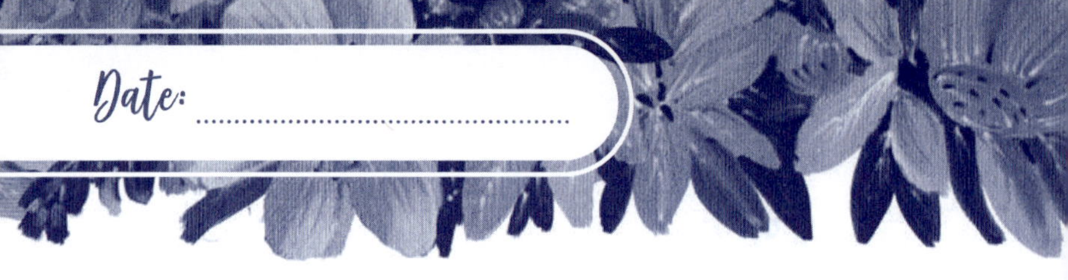

READ MATTHEW 6:24–34

"No one can serve two masters. For you will hate one and love the other; you will be devoted to one and despise the other. You cannot serve God and be enslaved to money. That is why I tell you not to worry about everyday life—whether you have enough food and drink, or enough clothes to wear. Isn't life more than food, and your body more than clothing?"

MATTHEW 6:24–25 NLT

Jesus, help me to bring my worries to You, trusting You to provide for me and leaving behind anything that isn't necessary. May I use money well for my own care and the care of others without letting it dominate my thoughts and desires. Amen.

prayer requests

praises

READ JOHN 15:1–11

"Remain in Me, and I in you. Just as the branch cannot bear fruit of itself but must remain in the vine, so neither can you unless you remain in Me. I am the vine, you are the branches; the one who remains in Me, and I in him bears much fruit, for apart from Me you can do nothing."

John 15:4–5 NASB

Jesus, You are my source of life and my hope for the abundant spiritual life You've promised. Help me to abide in You, remaining aware of Your presence and love so that I can bear the fruits of Your Spirit. Amen.

prayer requests

praises

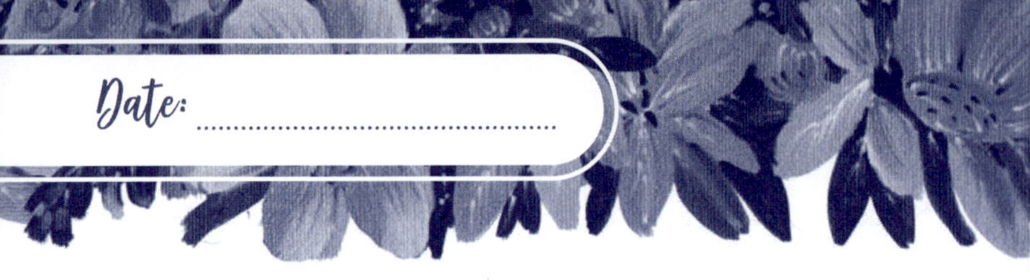

READ 1 JOHN 1:5–10

If we confess our sins, he is faithful and just and will forgive us our sins and purify us from all unrighteousness.

1 John 1:9 niv

Father, I come before You seeking Your forgiveness. I messed up. . .again. My sin creates a divide between You and me, and I can't bear it. Although I feel unworthy to ask, please purify my heart again. Cover me in Your grace and make me righteous before You. Amen.

prayer requests

praises

READ PSALM 147

The Lord's delight is in those who fear him,
those who put their hope in his unfailing love.
Psalm 147:11 NLT

Father, thank You for Your sustaining hope. I know I can trust You in all things, and that fact is a great source of comfort to me. I know difficult times will come, but I also know that Your love never fails. Help me to shine Your love and Your light of hope to people around me who may feel hopeless. You have not forgotten them. Amen.

prayer requests

praises

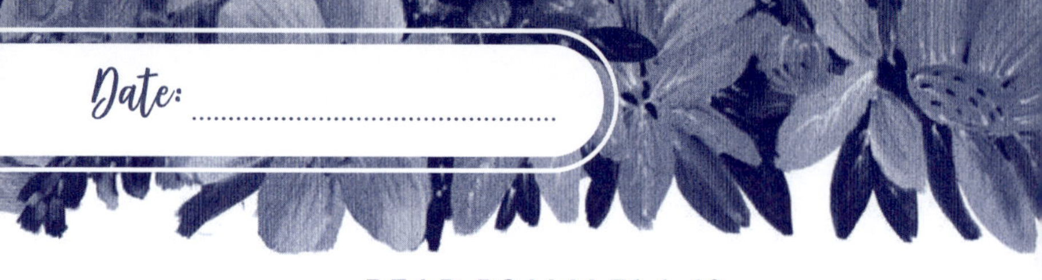

Date: ....

READ PSALM 71:1–12

In you, O Lord, I take refuge; let me never be put to shame. In your righteousness deliver me and rescue me; incline your ear to me and save me. Be to me a rock of refuge, a strong fortress, to save me, for you are my rock and my fortress. Rescue me, O my God, from the hand of the wicked, from the grasp of the unjust and cruel. For you, O Lord, are my hope, my trust, O Lord, from my youth.

Psalm 71:1–5 NRSV

Father, You are the true refuge in times of trouble and fear. I can trust that I am safe in Your care because of Your mercy and Your enduring love for me. May I turn away from every false sense of security and rely on You alone. Amen.

prayer requests

praises

READ HOSEA 2:14–23

"I will betroth you to Me forever; yes, I will betroth you to Me in righteousness and in justice, in favor and in compassion, and I will betroth you to Me in faithfulness. Then you will know the LORD."

HOSEA 2:19–20 NASB

Father, thank You for forgiving and restoring me so that I can move forward in faith and hope for the future. May I enjoy the peace You give Your faithful people. Amen.

prayer requests

praises

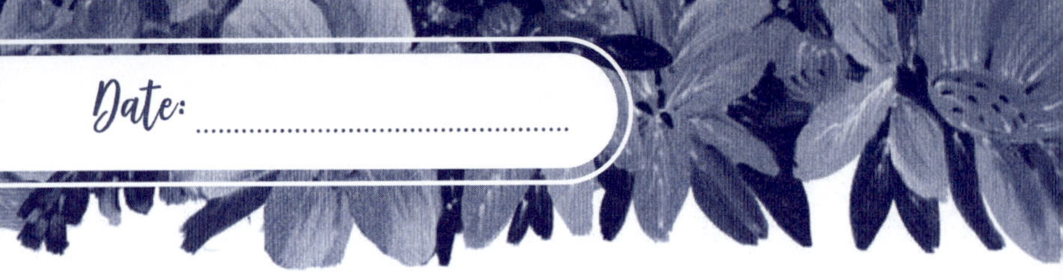

READ PSALM 19:1–6

The heavens are telling of the greatness of God and the great open spaces above show the work of His hands.

Psalm 19:1 NLV

Creator God, today I am celebrating Your artistry throughout all of Your creation. Even in nature around me every day, I can learn much about You. Give me Your eyes to appreciate and delight in the things You delight in. I praise You for the master artist You are. You have made all things good and pleasing in Your sight. Amen.

prayer requests

praises

READ PSALM 92

It is good to praise the Lord *and make music to your name, O Most High, proclaiming your love in the morning and your faithfulness at night.*

Psalm 92:1–2 niv

God of love, thank You for lavishing Your care and devotion on me. I am made whole in Your love. When I'm feeling unloved, unworthy, and forgotten today, wrap Your arms around me and remind me that I am Yours. Amen.

prayer requests

praises

READ ACTS 3:17–26

"Now, fellow Israelites, I know that you acted in ignorance, as did your leaders. But this is how God fulfilled what he had foretold through all the prophets, saying that his Messiah would suffer. Repent, then, and turn to God, so that your sins may be wiped out, that times of refreshing may come from the Lord."

Acts 3:17–19 NIV

Jesus, help me to remember the ways You have shown grace and mercy to me, freeing me from judgment of others. May I show the same patience and mercy to others so that they can enjoy times of refreshment. Amen.

prayer requests

praises

READ MATTHEW 25:14–30

"Then he ordered, 'Take the money from this servant, and give it to the one with the ten bags of silver. To those who use well what they are given, even more will be given, and they will have an abundance. But from those who do nothing, even what little they have will be taken away.'"

MATTHEW 25:28–29 NLT

Jesus, help me to recognize the talents You have given to me. Give me the strength and determination to use them well for Your purposes and to glorify You. Amen.

prayer requests

praises

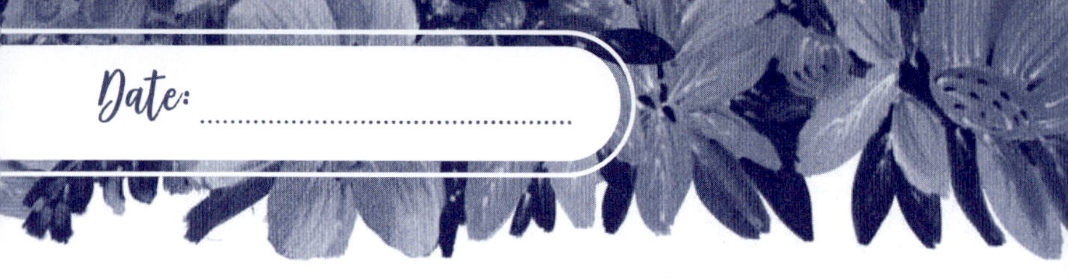

READ ROMANS 8:18–30

We know that God makes all things work together for the good of those who love Him and are chosen to be a part of His plan.

Romans 8:28 NLV

Good, good Father, thank You for Your promise that You're working all things together for my good. When I don't understand what You are doing, it's hard for me to wait, but still I hope. And I know my hope in You is never in vain. Give me patience to wait on Your timing and Your plan. Amen.

prayer requests

praises

READ PSALM 27

Wait patiently for the LORD. Be brave and courageous. Yes, wait patiently for the LORD.

PSALM 27:14 NLT

I don't like to wait, God. Even when I trust in Your perfect timing, I struggle. I worry. I fret. I want to take control of the situation and force my will. Give me patience. But today I'm also asking for courage. Make me brave to live in the confidence that You have this well under control and that You're lining up all the details for Your will to be done in my life. Amen.

prayer requests

praises

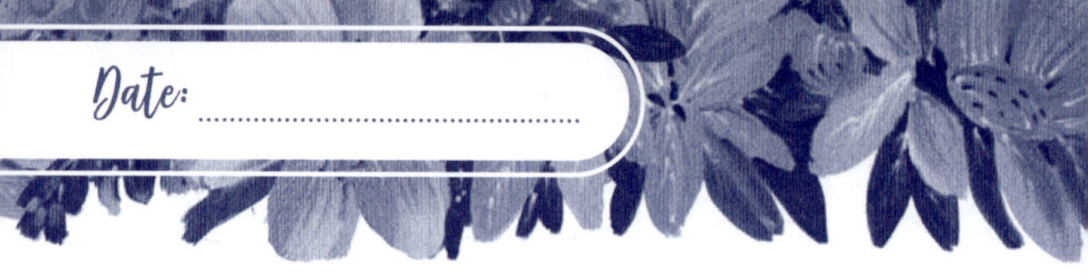

Date: ....

READ JONAH 3

"Who can tell? Perhaps even yet God will change his mind and hold back his fierce anger from destroying us."

JONAH 3:9 NLT

Lord, help me to remember that I am never far from mercy and restoration. May I always turn quickly to You after I have sinned so that I can receive Your mercy. May I show that same mercy to others who turn their hearts to You. Amen.

prayer requests

praises

READ COLOSSIANS 1:1–14

May you be made strong with all the strength that comes from his glorious power, and may you be prepared to endure everything with patience, while joyfully giving thanks to the Father, who has enabled you to share in the inheritance of the saints in the light.

COLOSSIANS 1:11–12 NRSV

Jesus, help me to endure the highs and lows of life with the strength and power You provide. May I keep in mind the hope of Your people who will one day share in Your inheritance because they relied on You above all else. Amen.

prayer requests

praises

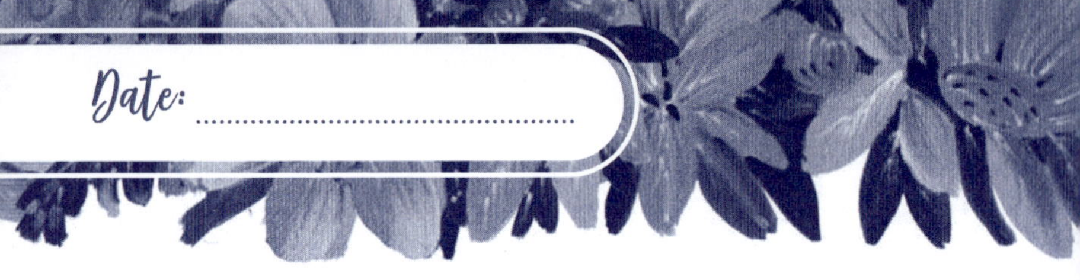

READ TITUS 3:3–8

When God our Savior revealed his kindness and love,
he saved us, not because of the righteous things we had done,
but because of his mercy. He washed away our sins,
giving us a new birth and new life through the Holy Spirit.

Titus 3:4–5 NLT

Father, when I think of all the ways You demonstrate how You love me, I realize just how kind You are to me. You bless me in so many ways, and You give me an identity in Christ that is perfect and whole—not dependent on my own goodness or abilities. Give me opportunities to show Your kindness to others today. Amen.

prayer requests

praises

READ PSALM 33:1–15

Let all the earth fear the LORD; let all the inhabitants of the world stand in awe of him!
PSALM 33:8 ESV

My Creator and King, show me the wonder of Your creation. In the life-giving nourishment of rainfall, in the majesty of a sunset, in the twinkling of points of light in the heavens, I am amazed. You provide everything I need, and what's more is You have made all things beautiful as well. Thank You, God. Amen.

prayer requests

praises

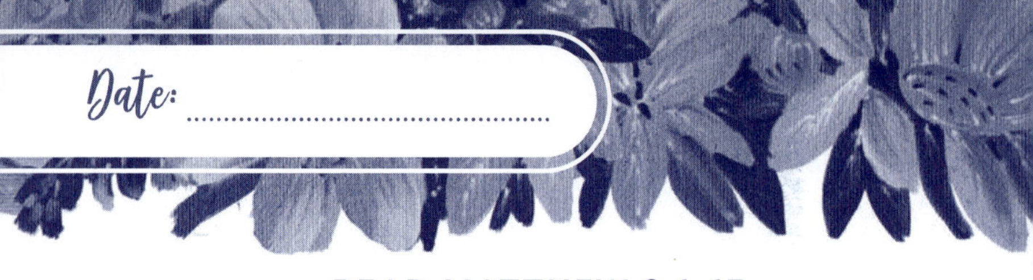

Date: ....

READ MATTHEW 8:1–13

But the officer said, "Lord, I am not worthy to have you come into my home. Just say the word from where you are, and my servant will be healed. I know this because I am under the authority of my superior officers, and I have authority over my soldiers. I only need to say, 'Go,' and they go, or 'Come,' and they come. And if I say to my slaves, 'Do this,' they do it."

MATTHEW 8:8–9 NLT

Jesus, You are all-powerful and fully able to answer my prayers, bringing healing and restoration to those in need. May I never take Your kindness and generosity for granted as I pray for myself and for others. Amen.

prayer requests

praises

READ ACTS 27:14–26

"And yet now I urge you to keep up your courage, for there will be no loss of life among you, but only of the ship. For this very night an angel of the God to whom I belong, whom I also serve, came to me, saying, 'Do not be afraid, Paul; you must stand before Caesar; and behold, God has graciously granted you all those who are sailing with you.' Therefore, keep up your courage, men, for I believe God that it will turn out exactly as I have been told."

Acts 27:22–25 NASB

Jesus, guide me in the choices I make today so that I won't fall into the trap of relying on my own wisdom. May I find Your path forward, and if I stray far from You, may I have the humility to correct my course. Amen.

prayer requests

praises

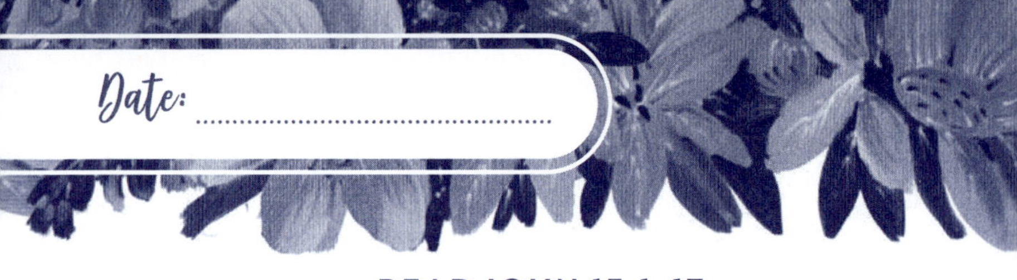

Date: ....

READ JOHN 15:1–17

"You didn't choose me. I chose you. I appointed you to go and produce lasting fruit, so that the Father will give you whatever you ask for, using my name."

JOHN 15:16 NLT

Jesus, "thank You" seems inadequate for my gratitude that You have chosen me. When others have turned their backs, I am confident that You never will. You are the vine, and I am the branch, and I will remain in You all my days. Thank You for remaining steadfast to the work of the Father. Amen.

prayer requests

praises

READ PSALM 46

"Be still, and know that I am God! I will be honored by every nation. I will be honored throughout the world."

Psalm 46:10 NLT

God, quiet my brain. I am here with You right now in body, mind, and spirit. You are God. You are good. You are holy. You are perfect. You are my rescuer, my Redeemer, my shepherd, my friend. I praise You for who You are. I praise You for all You do and all You have yet to do in the world and in my life. Amen.

prayer requests

praises

READ ISAIAH 43:14–25

Do not remember the former things, or consider the things of old. I am about to do a new thing; now it springs forth, do you not perceive it? I will make a way in the wilderness and rivers in the desert.

Isaiah 43:18–19 NRSV

Lord, help me to rely on Your power and wisdom and not on my own understanding or ability. May I look beyond what I know and what feels comfortable so that I can move into the new thing that You've called me to. Amen.

prayer requests

praises

READ 2 CORINTHIANS 7:2–12

Yet now I am happy, not because you were made sorry, but because your sorrow led you to repentance. For you became sorrowful as God intended and so were not harmed in any way by us. Godly sorrow brings repentance that leads to salvation and leaves no regret, but worldly sorrow brings death.

2 Corinthians 7:9–10 niv

Jesus, help me to both feel the weight of my sorrow over my sins and to move beyond my sorrow to the new life You offer as I repent. May I remember to show grace to those who are also moving through their sorrow and seeking Your renewal. Amen.

prayer requests

praises

READ 2 CORINTHIANS 12:1–10

Each time he said, "My grace is all you need. My power works best in weakness." So now I am glad to boast about my weaknesses, so that the power of Christ can work through me. That's why I take pleasure in my weaknesses, and in the insults, hardships, persecutions, and troubles that I suffer for Christ. For when I am weak, then I am strong.

2 Corinthians 12:9–10 NLT

God, when this world tells me to be empowered by my own strength, remind me that I am nothing without You. It feels strange to say it, but I thank You for my weak spots. Fill those gaps with Your power, dear Lord, and I will be strong in You today and forever. Amen.

prayer requests

praises

READ 2 CORINTHIANS 3:7–18

For the Lord is the Spirit, and wherever the Spirit of the Lord is, there is freedom. So all of us who have had that veil removed can see and reflect the glory of the Lord. And the Lord—who is the Spirit—makes us more and more like him as we are changed into his glorious image.

2 Corinthians 3:17–18 NLT

God, because of Jesus and the gift of Your Spirit, I know I live in freedom. Teach me how to live fully free and more like You each day. Amen.

prayer requests

praises

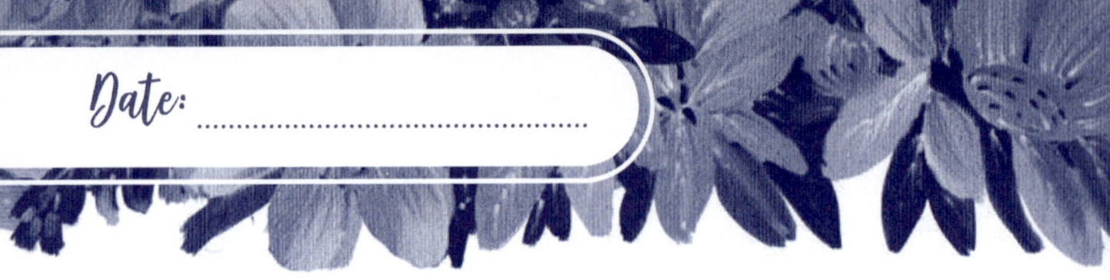

READ MATTHEW 18:21–35

" 'Shouldn't you have had mercy on your fellow servant just as I had on you?' In anger his master handed him over to the jailers to be tortured, until he should pay back all he owed. This is how my heavenly Father will treat each of you unless you forgive your brother or sister from your heart."

MATTHEW 18:33–35 NIV

Thank You, Lord, for the mercy You show in forgiving my debts and freeing me to serve You and others. May I show the same mercy and kindness to others so they can gain a glimpse of Your grace. Amen.

prayer requests

praises

READ ECCLESIASTES 9:7–18

The quiet words of the wise are more to be heeded than the shouts of a ruler of fools. Wisdom is better than weapons of war, but one sinner destroys much good.

Ecclesiastes 9:17–18 niv

Lord, I ask for the guidance of Your Holy Spirit to lead me forward in Your wisdom so that I will not fall into the trap of sin or the ignorance of my own judgments. May I remember the benefits of Your wisdom and seek it throughout my day today. Amen.

prayer requests

praises

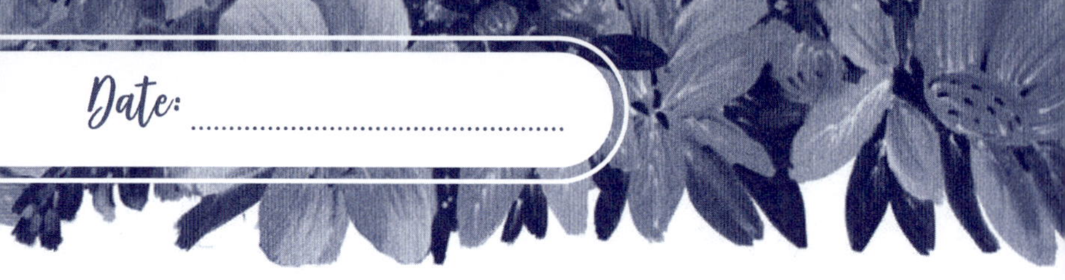

READ 1 CORINTHIANS 10:12–31

If you think you are standing strong, be careful not to fall. The temptations in your life are no different from what others experience. And God is faithful. He will not allow the temptation to be more than you can stand. When you are tempted, he will show you a way out so that you can endure.

1 Corinthians 10:12–13 nlt

God, I know when I am tempted to sin that temptation doesn't come from You—it comes from my own selfish desires. Help me to recognize the areas in which I am most vulnerable to temptation and deliver on Your promise that You will show me an exit to avoid the temptation. Amen.

prayer requests

praises

READ PSALM 119:1–16

How can a young person stay on the path of purity? By living according to your word. I seek you with all my heart; do not let me stray from your commands. I have hidden your word in my heart that I might not sin against you.

Psalm 119:9–11 NIV

Almighty Lord, I am grateful for Your Word. Let Your scripture take root in my heart and soul. Help me to commit more and more of Your wisdom to memory, and let it come to mind when I need it and when I can encourage someone else. Amen.

prayer requests

praises

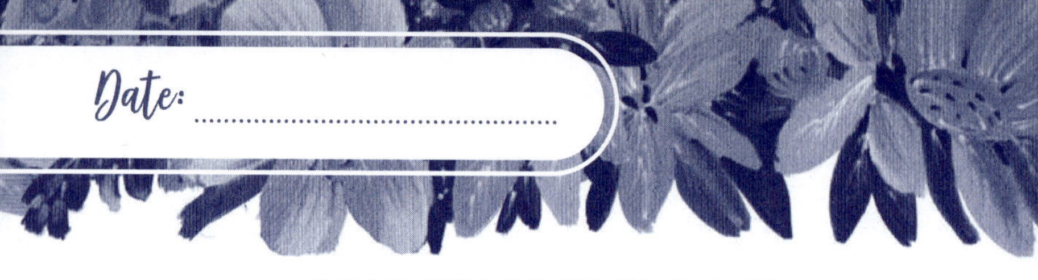

READ COLOSSIANS 2:6–15

As you therefore have received Christ Jesus the Lord, continue to live your lives in him, rooted and built up in him and established in the faith, just as you were taught, abounding in thanksgiving. See to it that no one takes you captive through philosophy and empty deceit, according to human tradition, according to the elemental spirits of the universe, and not according to Christ.

COLOSSIANS 2:6–8 NRSV

Jesus, thank You for receiving me and connecting me with the Father so that I can live by faith in Your care, love, and power. May I continue to rely on You and not any other foundation. Amen.

prayer requests

praises

READ 1 JOHN 3

We know what real love is because Jesus gave up his life for us. So we also ought to give up our lives for our brothers and sisters. If someone has enough money to live well and sees a brother or sister in need but shows no compassion—how can God's love be in that person?

1 John 3:16–17 NLT

Thank You, Father, for Your deep love for me and for the sacrifice of Jesus on my behalf. Thank You for seeking me when I was far from You. May Your love transform my life and enable me to more fully love others. Amen.

prayer requests

praises

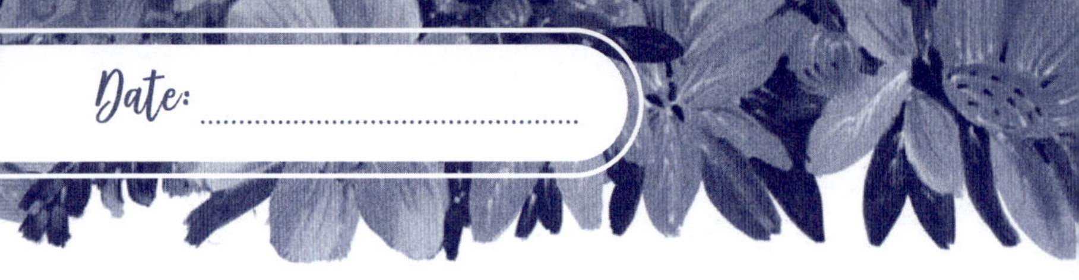

READ PSALM 118

This is the day the LORD has made. We will rejoice and be glad in it.

PSALM 118:24 NLT

God, today I am choosing joy. Not because everything is perfect and not because I feel overly happy. I'm choosing to rejoice because today is a day You made. And I know it is good because You are good. Thank You for loving me today and every day. Thank You for giving me a reason to rejoice! Amen.

prayer requests

praises

READ DEUTERONOMY 7:6–9

Know therefore that the LORD your God is God; he is the faithful God, keeping his covenant of love to a thousand generations of those who love him and keep his commandments.

DEUTERONOMY 7:9 NIV

Father God, I praise You because of Your faithfulness. You are my rock and my strong fortress that cannot be moved. I don't have to fretfully wonder what You're doing in my life because I trust You fully. Infuse my spirit with steadfastness in my relationships. I want to shine Your light of faithfulness to others in everyday life. Amen.

prayer requests

praises

READ MATTHEW 15:21–31

She replied, "That's true, Lord, but even dogs are allowed to eat the scraps that fall beneath their masters' table." "Dear woman," Jesus said to her, "your faith is great. Your request is granted." And her daughter was instantly healed.

MATTHEW 15:27–28 NLT

Jesus, thank You for hearing my prayers and honoring my humble perseverance. Help me to continue to pray in faith for myself and for others so that we can draw closer to You and enjoy relief from our struggles in this world. Amen.

prayer requests

praises

READ PHILIPPIANS 1:12–20

What then? Only that in every way, whether in pretense or in truth, Christ is proclaimed, and in this I rejoice. But not only that, I also will rejoice, for I know that this will turn out for my deliverance through your prayers and the provision of the Spirit of Jesus Christ.

PHILIPPIANS 1:18–19 NASB

Jesus, help me to leave behind my desire for an easy life so that I can better advance the cause of Your kingdom and share Your message boldly with others. Amen.

prayer requests

praises

READ 1 JOHN 5:13–20

This is the confidence we have in approaching God: that if we ask anything according to his will, he hears us. And if we know that he hears us—whatever we ask— we know that we have what we asked of him.

1 John 5:14–15 niv

Father, I am confident in my prayers to You. Give me Your wisdom to approach You with requests that You will hear and grant. I long to be in the center of Your good and perfect plan, God. Amen.

prayer requests

praises

READ PSALM 37:1–9

Take delight in the Lord, and he will give you the desires of your heart.

Psalm 37:4 NIV

Lord, You fill me with such joy. Today my heart is singing as I delight in You. You are a good, good Father who gives me care, compassion, and kindness every day. Because of You, I have everything I need. Let my heart draw close to Yours, Father. I praise You because of who You are. Amen.

prayer requests

praises

READ JOHN 17:1–19

"I am not asking you to take them out of the world, but I ask you to protect them from the evil one. They do not belong to the world, just as I do not belong to the world. Sanctify them in the truth; your word is truth. As you have sent me into the world, so I have sent them into the world."

John 17:15–18 NRSV

Jesus, I ask for Your protection, transformation, and guidance as I go out into the world to share the hope of Your message with others. Help me to view others with compassion and mercy so that I can be an effective ambassador for You. Amen.

prayer requests

praises

READ JOHN 15:12–17

"You did not choose Me but I chose you, and appointed you that you would go and bear fruit, and that your fruit would remain, so that whatever you ask of the Father in My name He may give to you. This I command you, that you love one another."

John 15:16–17 NASB

Thank You, Father, for the incredible access You have granted to me through Your Son, Jesus. May my prayers remain in line with the will of Jesus, and may I bear fruit that endures for years to the benefit of many. Amen.

prayer requests

praises

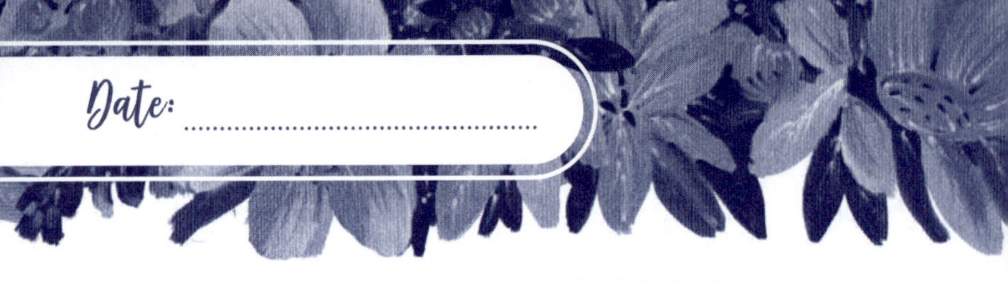

READ MATTHEW 6:1–4

"But when you give to the needy, do not let your left hand know what your right hand is doing, so that your giving may be in secret. Then your Father, who sees what is done in secret, will reward you."

Matthew 6:3–4 niv

Generous God, thank You for the ability to give to others—to meet real needs in Your name. Show me opportunities to give in secret and keep my motives pure so that I'm not seeking praise or glory for myself. Everything I have is from You, Father. I am so blessed. Amen.

prayer requests

praises

READ PROVERBS 3:1–12

Trust in the LORD with all your heart; do not depend on your own understanding. Seek his will in all you do, and he will show you which path to take.

PROVERBS 3:5–6 NLT

Lord God, I admit there are times I'd rather trust my gut than trust You. When I'm in danger of relying on my own wits to make a decision, remind me that Your will is what I want to follow. Make Your path obvious and cleared of obstacles so that I will walk confidently ahead. Be the King of my heart today and every day, Father. Amen.

prayer requests

praises

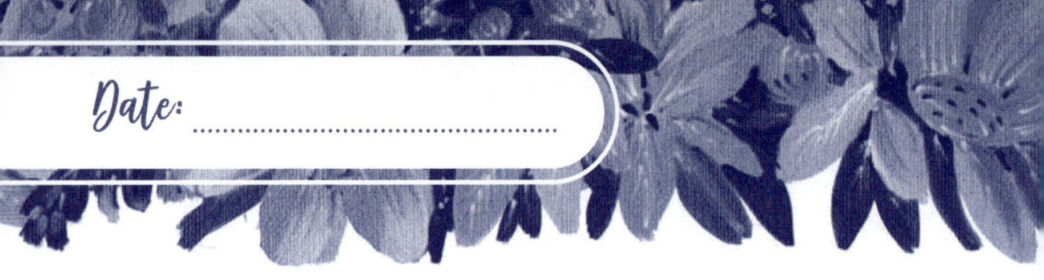

READ 1 CORINTHIANS 13

Three things will last forever—faith, hope, and love—and the greatest of these is love.

1 Corinthians 13:13 NLT

Jesus, help me to put the lesser pursuits of spiritual gifts, prophecies, and knowledge in their proper places so that I can see the purity and power of Your love. May I receive Your love and then share it widely with others. Amen.

prayer requests

praises

READ 2 TIMOTHY 2:14–25

And the Lord's servant must not be quarrelsome but must be kind to everyone, able to teach, not resentful. Opponents must be gently instructed, in the hope that God will grant them repentance leading them to a knowledge of the truth.

2 Timothy 2:24–25 NIV

Jesus, help me to pursue the best for everyone I meet, especially those who oppose me or who may be in error. Help me to speak with gentleness and humility with others so that I can bring them closer to You and Your truth. Amen.

prayer requests

praises

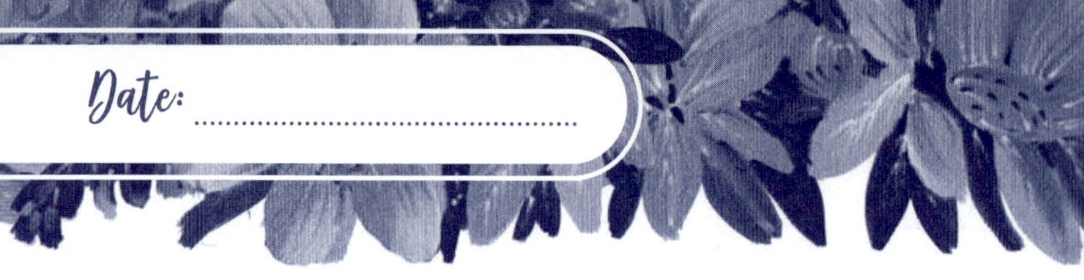

READ ZEPHANIAH 3:14–20

"Do not fear, Zion; do not let your hands hang limp. The LORD your God is with you, the Mighty Warrior who saves. He will take great delight in you; in his love he will no longer rebuke you, but will rejoice over you with singing."

ZEPHANIAH 3:16–17 NIV

Defender God, thank You for saving me. I praise You for the strength You instill in me. Today I will lift my head and raise my hands in Your victory even in the midst of my struggles. I delight in You, Father. Your ways are good and perfect, so please lead me today. Amen.

prayer requests

praises

READ JOHN 3:16–21

"For this is how God loved the world: He gave his one and only Son, so that everyone who believes in him will not perish but have eternal life."

JOHN 3:16 NLT

Merciful Father, Your love is rooted in the most giving, unselfish act in all of history. As difficult as it was for Jesus to lay down His own life, how much harder must it have been for You to give up Your beloved Son to be a human sacrifice. Thank You for loving the world so much that You made a way when there was no other way. Amen.

prayer requests

praises

Date:

READ MATTHEW 20:1–16

"He answered one of them, 'Friend, I haven't been unfair! Didn't you agree to work all day for the usual wage? Take your money and go. I wanted to pay this last worker the same as you. Is it against the law for me to do what I want with my money? Should you be jealous because I am kind to others?'"

Matthew 20:13–15 NLT

Jesus, help me to remember the ways You have generously forgiven me and shown me mercy so that I am grateful to You and compassionate toward others. Amen.

prayer requests

praises

READ JOHN 6:25–40

"For the bread of God is that which comes down from heaven and gives life to the world." They said to him, "Sir, give us this bread always." Jesus said to them, "I am the bread of life. Whoever comes to me will never be hungry, and whoever believes in me will never be thirsty."

JOHN 6:33–35 NRSV

Jesus, help me to move past the distractions that draw me away from the fulfillment and restoration You offer. May I find satisfaction in You and in the spiritual sustenance You offer. Amen.

prayer requests

praises

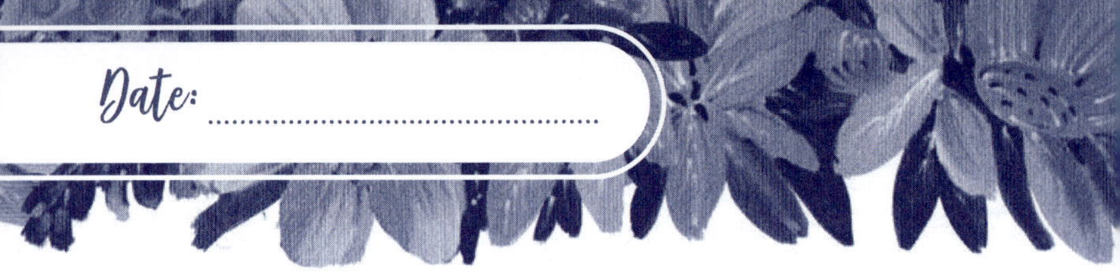

READ ISAIAH 43:1–13

"Do not be afraid, for I have ransomed you.
I have called you by name; you are mine."
Isaiah 43:1 NLT

God, when I read Isaiah 43, I am overwhelmed by Your kindness to me. You tell me I am precious to You and You love me. You remind me again and again that You are with me no matter what and that I have nothing to fear. Forgive me when I forget these truths. Write them on my heart so I will always find my security in You. Amen.

prayer requests

praises

READ 1 PETER 1:13–19

For you know that God paid a ransom to save you from the empty life you inherited from your ancestors. And it was not paid with mere gold or silver, which lose their value. It was the precious blood of Christ, the sinless, spotless Lamb of God.

1 PETER 1:18–19 NLT

Jesus, when I think of how Your precious blood paid the ransom for my life, I am humbled to the point of tears. I don't deserve such generosity, such love, such grace. But You willingly went to the cross to finish the nasty business of Satan's claim on my soul. My heart is Yours. My soul is Yours. Make me more like You. Amen.

prayer requests

praises

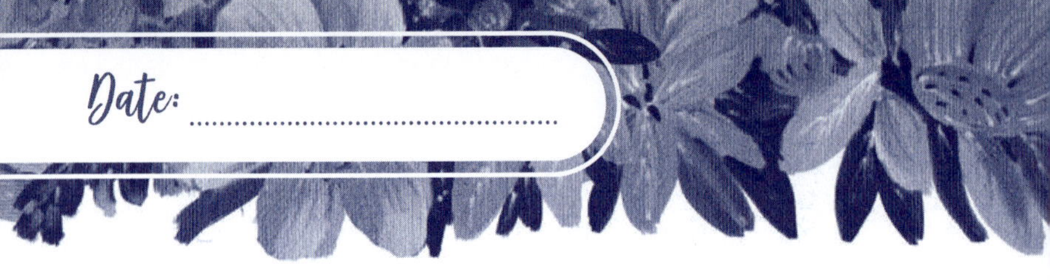

READ JEREMIAH 17:5–12

"But blessed is the one who trusts in the Lord, whose confidence is in him. They will be like a tree planted by the water that sends out its roots by the stream. It does not fear when heat comes; its leaves are always green. It has no worries in a year of drought and never fails to bear fruit."

Jeremiah 17:7–8 niv

Lord, I look to You as my source of stability, direction, and joy. Help me to remain rooted in You so that I am not blown about by the shifting winds of life. May I rest in the confidence of Your reward, which is coming one day. Amen.

prayer requests

praises

READ LUKE 22:24–38

"But I have pleaded in prayer for you, Simon, that your faith should not fail. So when you have repented and turned to me again, strengthen your brothers." Peter said, "Lord, I am ready to go to prison with you, and even to die with you."

LUKE 22:32–33 NLT

Jesus, help me to view my weaknesses with honesty and clarity so that I can remain careful and attentive while also trusting You to support me when I'm struggling. Amen.

prayer requests

praises

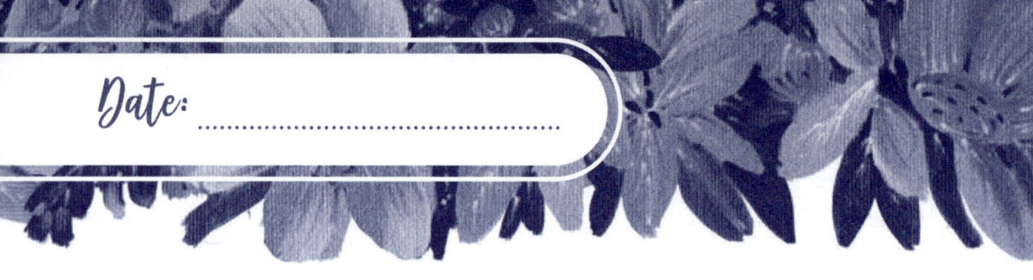

Date:

READ EPHESIANS 2:1–10

For by His loving-favor you have been saved from the punishment of sin through faith. It is not by anything you have done. It is a gift of God.

EPHESIANS 2:8 NLV

Life-giving God, I am so thankful for Your gift of salvation. It's a gift that seems too good to be true, yet Your promises never fail, and I have full confidence that I am saved by Your grace. Help me to lead others to accept Your gift, Father. Give me the words and actions that show Your loving-kindness to everyone around me. Amen.

prayer requests

praises

READ PSALM 23

Yes, even if I walk through the valley of the shadow of death,
I will not be afraid of anything, because You are with me.

Psalm 23:4 nlv

God, I feel alone. But my feelings often can't be trusted. My head and heart know that You are here. You are my watchful shepherd, and I am Your beloved lamb. Guide me through the dark valleys of life. And please use Your staff to keep me on the path with You. I do not want to stray from Your loving presence. Amen.

prayer requests

praises

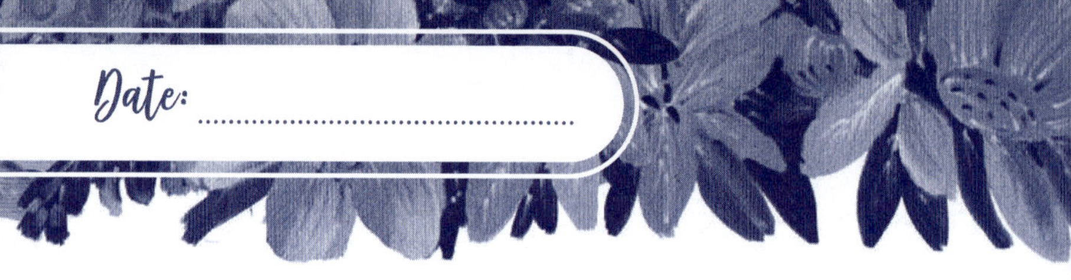

Date: ....

READ 1 TIMOTHY 2:1–15

I urge, then, first of all, that petitions, prayers, intercession and thanksgiving be made for all people—for kings and all those in authority, that we may live peaceful and quiet lives in all godliness and holiness.

1 Timothy 2:1–2 niv

Father, my soul longs for peaceful unity, but politically I feel none. Give me Your heart for the leaders and people in authority of my town, my state, and my nation. Press upon my spirit a name or two that You want me to specifically pray for. Give them pure hearts to lead well and do what is right in Your eyes. Amen.

prayer requests

praises

READ 1 PETER 4:1–11

Above all, maintain constant love for one another, for love covers a multitude of sins. Be hospitable to one another without complaining. Like good stewards of the manifold grace of God, serve one another with whatever gift each of you has received.

1 Peter 4:8–10 NRSV

Jesus, help me to see the love, grace, and favor You have given to me. May I recognize Your gifts and freely share them with others, disciplining myself to pray and to love others with generosity. Amen.

prayer requests

praises

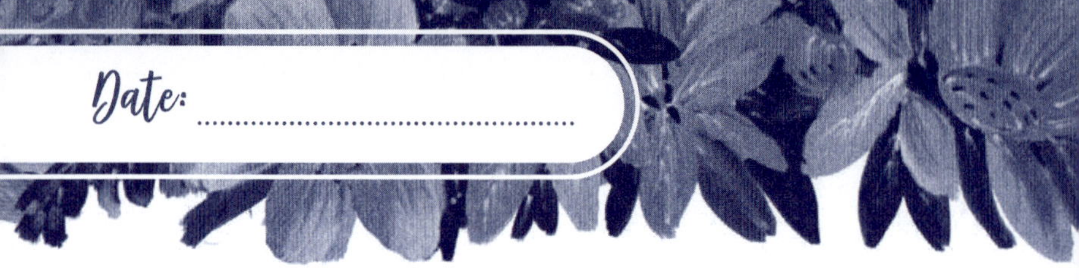

Date: ....

READ GENESIS 1:1–31

God saw all that he had made, and it was very good. And there was evening, and there was morning—the sixth day.

Genesis 1:31 niv

Heavenly Father, You have made all things. You are the Creator who sustains life. You knit me together in my mother's womb. May I treat with great respect all of Your creation, even that which others may devalue. Amen.

prayer requests

praises

READ EPHESIANS 1:3–14

God decided in advance to adopt us into his own family by bringing us to himself through Jesus Christ. This is what he wanted to do, and it gave him great pleasure.

Ephesians 1:5 NLT

Father, I am overwhelmed when I consider the fact that You see me as worthy of being Your adopted, chosen daughter. Because of my brother, Jesus, You see me as holy and blameless. I don't deserve such favor, but I gratefully accept it. Amen.

prayer requests

praises

READ 2 TIMOTHY 1:3–11

I remember your genuine faith, for you share the faith that first filled your grandmother Lois and your mother, Eunice. And I know that same faith continues strong in you.

2 Timothy 1:5 NLT

Father, thank You for the heritage of faith in my life. I am humbled when I think about the people who loved me so much that they led me to Your Son. I want to pass on the legacy of Your goodness and salvation to the next generation. Show me who. Show me how. Give me Your heart. Amen.

prayer requests

praises

READ EXODUS 3:1–22

Moses said to God, "Suppose I go to the Israelites and say to them, 'The God of your fathers has sent me to you,' and they ask me, 'What is his name?' Then what shall I tell them?" God said to Moses, "I AM WHO I AM. This is what you are to say to the Israelites: 'I AM has sent me to you.'"

EXODUS 3:13–14 NIV

Great I AM, I humbly ask You to take the reins and lead me day to day, step by step through life, just as You led Your people out of slavery in the land of Egypt. Amen.

prayer requests

praises

Date: ....

READ PSALMS 130:1–132:18

I wait for the LORD, my whole being waits,
and in his word I put my hope.
PSALM 130:5 NIV

Lord, as I wait, please help me to know that Your timing is always right for me. You always have my best interest at heart. In the waiting, help me to claim Your promises and to trust in Your Word. Amen.

prayer requests

praises

READ EPHESIANS 1:15–23

I pray that your hearts will be flooded with light so that you can understand the confident hope he has given to those he called—his holy people who are his rich and glorious inheritance.

Ephesians 1:18 NLT

Jesus, You are the light of the world. Shine on me today. Holy Spirit, You are my helper. Move in my heart today. God, You are my mighty defender. Walk ahead of me today and be victorious over the struggles and frustrations and roadblocks that will come my way. Amen.

prayer requests

praises

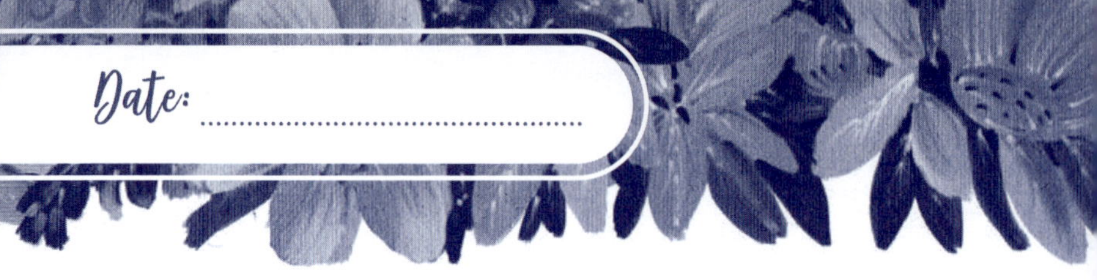

READ ISAIAH 50:4–9

Because the Sovereign LORD helps me, I will not be disgraced. Therefore have I set my face like flint, and I know I will not be put to shame.

ISAIAH 50:7 NIV

Father, I admit that sometimes I don't act because I fear how it will be perceived by others. Forgive me for not trusting that You will keep me from being disgraced. When all is said and done, I know what You think of me is all that matters, but I want to be liked, respected, and accepted by everyone. Show me Your will in all things. Amen.

prayer requests

praises

READ DEUTERONOMY 31:1–30

"Do not be afraid or discouraged, for the LORD will personally go ahead of you. He will be with you; he will neither fail you nor abandon you."

DEUTERONOMY 31:8 NLT

Heavenly Father, I will go where You lead. Help me to lay down fear and worry. I want to trade those hindrances in for Your help and Your faithfulness. I know that You go before me. Wherever You may lead, I will follow in faith. Amen.

prayer requests

praises

READ JOSHUA 1:1–18

"This book of the Law shall not depart from your mouth, but you shall meditate on it day and night, so that you may be careful to do according to all that is written in it; for then you will make your way prosperous, and then you will achieve success.

JOSHUA 1:8 NASB

God, thank You for Your holy Word. These verses remind me how important it is that I do not just leave my Bible in the car after church on Sunday but that I spend time in it daily. Your Word is my pathway to success, and I want to honor You by doing what it says. Amen.

prayer requests

praises

READ PHILIPPIANS 4:10–20

I know how to live on almost nothing or with everything. I have learned the secret of living in every situation, whether it is with a full stomach or empty, with plenty or little. For I can do everything through Christ, who gives me strength.

PHILIPPIANS 4:12–13 NLT

God, I admit that I struggle with being content. My selfishness always seems to compare my situation with someone who has a little bit more. Forgive me for being ungrateful for all You provide. Teach me to be content in any situation, and if ends aren't meeting, give me the faith to trust that You will provide. Because I know You will. Amen.

prayer requests

praises

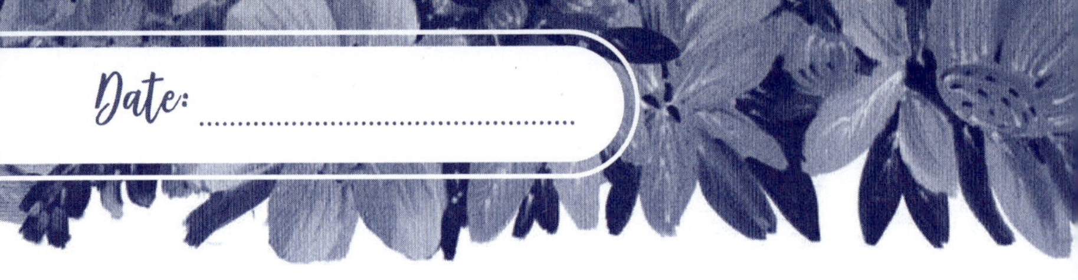

Date: ....

READ PSALM 103:8–18

For as high as the heavens are above the earth, so great is his love for those who fear him; as far as the east is from the west, so far has he removed our transgressions from us.

Psalm 103:11–12 niv

Father God, I already know I am forgiven, and I believe it when scripture says that You have removed my sins as far as the east is from the west. But I still feel guilt over the past, and I can't seem to shake it. Please take my guilt as far away as my sins. Amen.

prayer requests

praises

READ JUDGES 13:1–25

[Manoah] said to his wife, "We will certainly die, for we have seen God!" But his wife said, "If the Lord were going to kill us, he wouldn't have accepted our burnt offering and grain offering. He wouldn't have appeared to us and told us this wonderful thing and done these miracles."

Judges 13:22–23 NLT

Lord, help me not to be the one who panics and overreacts in my family. Use me as a source of calm and reason. I want to trust You in all things. Every day has enough worry of its own. Help me to walk in trust that You always have the best interest of my loved ones and myself in mind. Amen.

prayer requests

praises

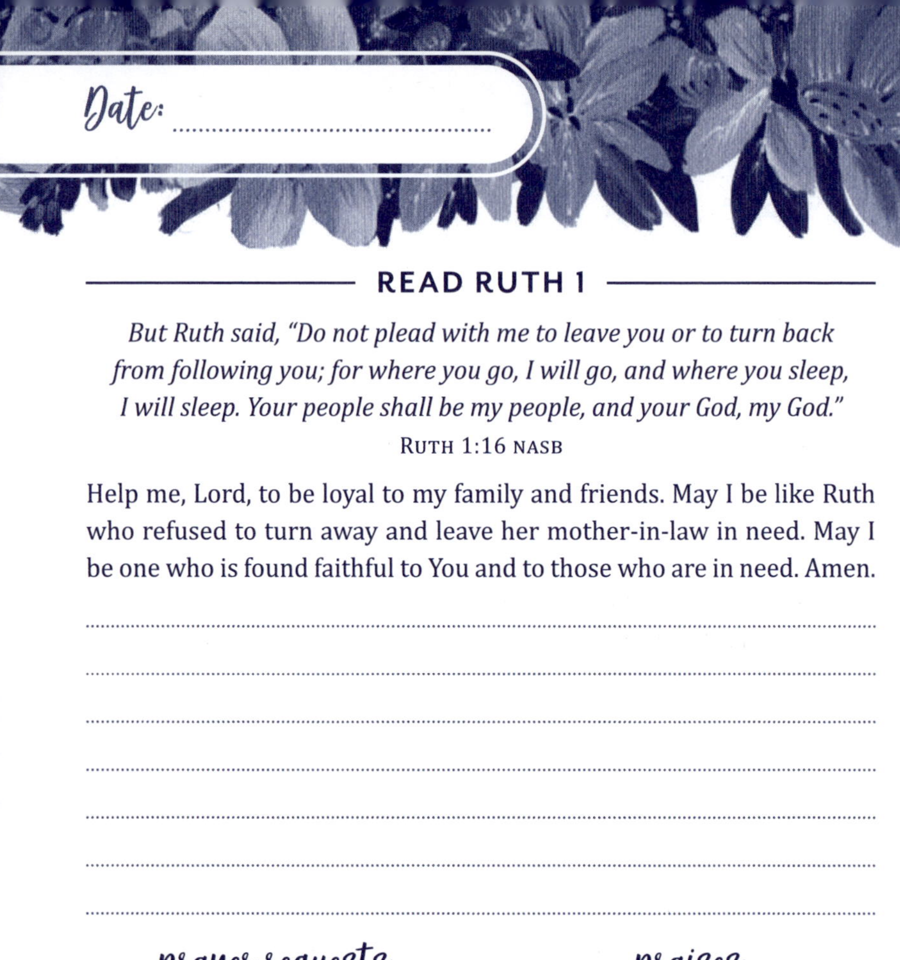

READ RUTH 1

But Ruth said, "Do not plead with me to leave you or to turn back from following you; for where you go, I will go, and where you sleep, I will sleep. Your people shall be my people, and your God, my God."

RUTH 1:16 NASB

Help me, Lord, to be loyal to my family and friends. May I be like Ruth who refused to turn away and leave her mother-in-law in need. May I be one who is found faithful to You and to those who are in need. Amen.

prayer requests

praises

READ ISAIAH 43:14–21

"For I am about to do something new. See, I have already begun! Do you not see it? I will make a pathway through the wilderness. I will create rivers in the dry wasteland."

Isaiah 43:19 NLT

I'm ready for change, God. Lead me through this wilderness to Your promised land. Show me what You will have me do. Amen.

prayer requests

praises

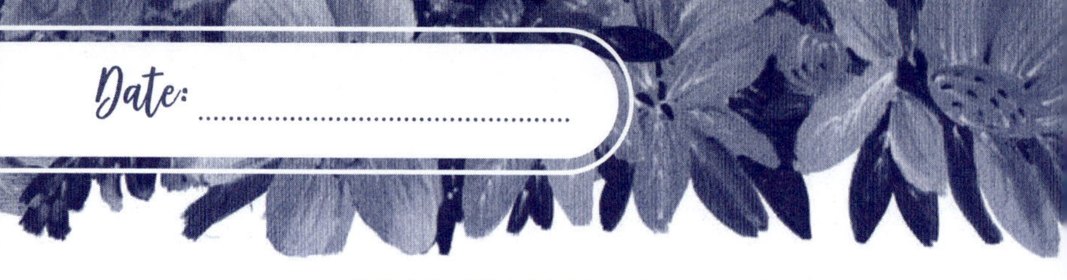

Date: ....

READ ISAIAH 40:22–31

He gives strength to the weary and increases the power of the weak. Even youths grow tired and weary, and young men stumble and fall; but those who hope in the Lord will renew their strength. They will soar on wings like eagles; they will run and not grow weary, they will walk and not be faint.

Isaiah 40:29–31 niv

God, I have so many dreams and goals, but sometimes I don't know where to begin. Show me what You want for me and set me on the path toward those goals. Put the drive and tenacity in my heart to make them happen. I give You all the glory for any success I will have. Amen.

prayer requests

praises

READ 1 SAMUEL 1:1–28

"I asked the Lord to give me this boy, and he has granted my request. Now I am giving him to the Lord, and he will belong to the Lord his whole life." And they worshiped the Lord there.

1 Samuel 1:27–28 NLT

Heavenly Father, You know my deepest longings and desires. Mold my heart and mind so that I will think like You and desire only that which will bring You glory. Like Hannah, help me to honor You with all the good gifts You pour into my life. Amen.

prayer requests

praises

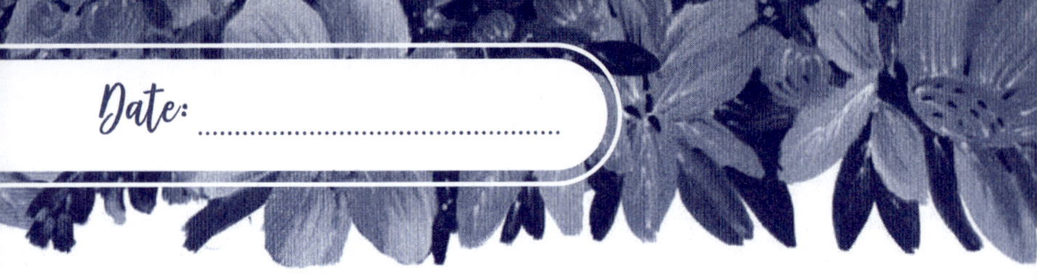

READ ECCLESIASTES 3

There is a time for everything, and a season
for every activity under the heavens.
ECCLESIASTES 3:1 NIV

Heavenly Father, help me to know how to react to change in my life. Guide me as I seek to find the balance between laughter and sorrow, rejoicing and mourning. Life is an adventure. Thank You for being with me in every time and in every season. Amen.

prayer requests

praises

READ LAMENTATIONS 3:22–33

Because of the Lord*'s great love we are not consumed, for his compassions never fail. They are new every morning; great is your faithfulness.*

Lamentations 3:22–23 niv

Merciful Father, today I seek Your refreshing forgiveness. I had every intention of perfection yesterday, but I messed up again. I'm ashamed of my sin, but I'm choosing to look up to You and admit I need Your kind compassion every day. I dedicate this new day to You, God. And I will live it as Your imperfect child who is perfectly loved by You. Amen.

prayer requests

praises

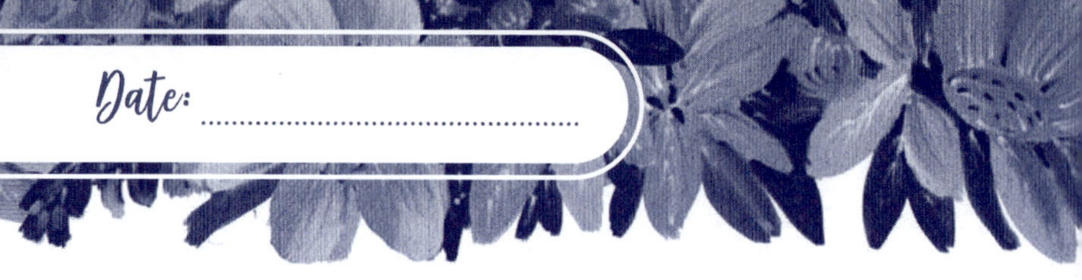

Date: ....

READ ISAIAH 55:6–13

"For My thoughts are not your thoughts, and My ways are not your ways," says the Lord. "For as the heavens are higher than the earth, so are My ways higher than your ways, and My thoughts than your thoughts."

Isaiah 55:8–9 NLV

Lord God, sometimes Your ways are a complete mystery to me. I don't understand what You're doing, and I realize—yet again—that I'm not in control. But the truth is, I am thankful Your ways and plans are better, more holy, and absolutely perfect. So even when I don't understand, lead on. Amen.

prayer requests

praises

READ 1 SAMUEL 17

And David said, "The LORD who saved me from the paw of the lion and the paw of the bear, He will save me from the hand of this Philistine." And Saul said to David, "Go, and may the LORD be with you."

1 SAMUEL 17:37 NASB

Lord, thank You for the times You have protected me and provided a way of escape. You have built up in me a confidence that next time and the time after that, You will remain faithful. You will show up. Help me to trust in Your strength as You continue to use me and to put challenges in my path. Amen.

prayer requests

praises

READ 2 KINGS 4

She said to her husband, "I know that this man who often comes our way is a holy man of God. Let's make a small room on the roof and put in it a bed and a table, a chair and a lamp for him. Then he can stay there whenever he comes to us."

2 Kings 4:9–10 niv

Lord, all of my resources come straight from Your hand. Nothing that I own—my home, my car, even the food in my pantry—belongs to me. It is all on loan from You. Please show me opportunities to use my resources to meet the needs of those around me. Make me hospitable and kind like the Shunammite woman. Amen.

prayer requests

praises

READ REVELATION 21:1–8

"He will wipe away every tear from their eyes, and death shall be no more, neither shall there be mourning, nor crying, nor pain anymore, for the former things have passed away."

REVELATION 21:4 ESV

Heavenly Father, I am so thankful for the confidence I have in an eternity with You. I can't fathom the wonders that Your creative hand has in store for the new heaven and the new earth, and I can't wait to see Your masterful work! I long for that renewal personally too. Make me new today; change me to be more like You. Amen.

prayer requests

praises

READ LUKE 6:27–35

"I say to you who hear Me, love those who work against you. Do good to those who hate you. Respect and give thanks for those who try to bring bad to you. Pray for those who make it very hard for you."

LUKE 6:27–28 NLV

This is a hard one, God. I receive no respect, so everything inside me wants to disrespect in return. And love them? Do good to them? I can't do this on my own, Father. Inhabit this relationship. Give me Your eyes to see them the way You see them. That's the only way I will be able to love. Amen.

prayer requests

praises

READ ESTHER 4:1–17

"If you keep quiet at a time like this, deliverance and relief for the Jews will arise from some other place, but you and your relatives will die. Who knows if perhaps you were made queen for just such a time as this?"

ESTHER 4:14 NLT

Lord, help me to be like Esther as I take risks for Your Kingdom. Help me to trust You as she did when she went before the king, knowing that he could choose to end her life. I want to do Your will in my life regardless of the risk. I long to be a part of Your plans. Amen.

prayer requests

praises

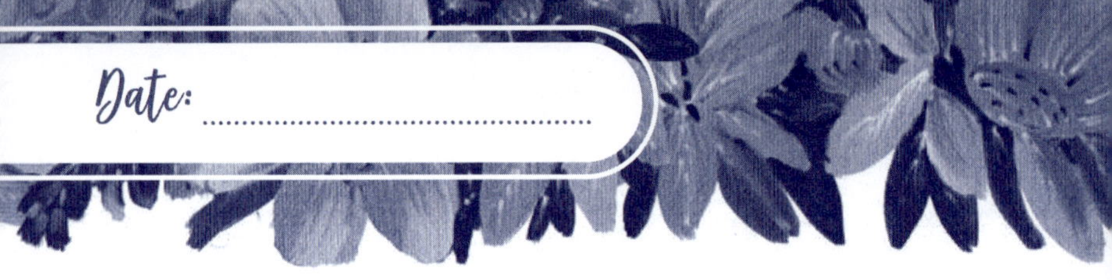

READ PSALMS 27:1–28:9

Wait for the LORD; be strong and let your heart take courage; yes, wait for the LORD.

PSALM 27:14 NASB

Lord, when I do not feel You near, remind me that You promise never to leave or forsake me. You are my protector and provider. I will praise You all the days of my life. Help me to wait well when I am required to do so. Amen.

prayer requests

praises

READ COLOSSIANS 3:1–14

Therefore, as God's chosen people, holy and dearly loved,
clothe yourselves with compassion, kindness,
humility, gentleness and patience.
Colossians 3:12 NIV

God, I want to be more like You. You shower me with compassion and kindness. But my own selfishness gets in the way of being like You—I am proud and impatient with others. Help me to realize how much I have been forgiven, how much You love me, so that I can show this same love to others. Amen.

prayer requests

praises

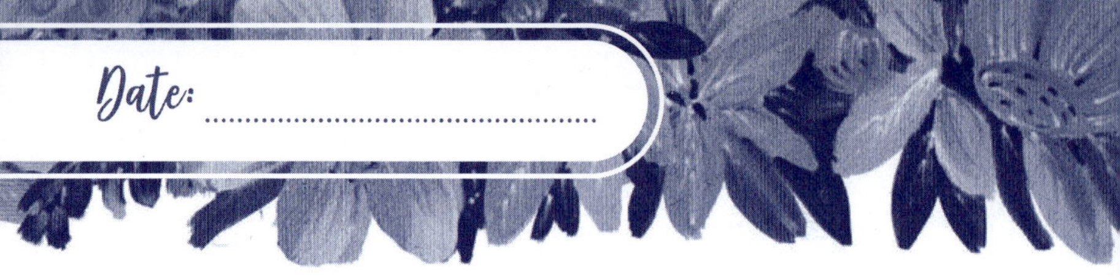

READ 1 THESSALONIANS 5:12–22

Always be joyful. Never stop praying. Be thankful in all circumstances, for this is God's will for you who belong to Christ Jesus.

1 Thessalonians 5:16–18 nlt

Father, I admit that sometimes my joy gets buried deep under the daily stresses of life. Restore to me my joy in You. Today I will pray to You with every breath I take. And I will find new joy in You in every circumstance—not just the happy ones but in all circumstances. Thank You for loving me. Thank You for choosing me. Thank You for leading me in Your goodness. Amen.

prayer requests

praises